THE
FURNITURE
PAINTING
KIT

THE
FURNITURE
PAINTING
KIT

Belinda Ballantine

Photography by Sue Atkinson

Little, Brown and Company
Boston • New York • Toronto • London

For my darling daughters Antonia and Georgie,
and Moley my most special canine companion.

A LITTLE, BROWN BOOK

First published in Great Britain in 1995
by Little, Brown and Company (UK)

Text and designs copyright © Belinda Ballantine 1995
Photographs copyright © Sue Atkinson 1995 (except pages 8 and 9)
This edition copyright © Eddison Sadd Editions 1995

A CIP catalogue record for this book is available from the British Library.

ISBN 0-316-91067-8

1 3 5 7 9 8 6 4 2

AN EDDISON·SADD EDITION
Edited, designed and produced by
Eddison Sadd Editions Limited
St Chad's Court
146B King's Cross Road
London WC1X 9DH

Phototypeset in ITC Modern No. 216 by Dorchester Typesetting Group UK.
Colour origination by Sele & Color, Italy.
Produced by Mandarin Offset, printed and bound in Hong Kong.

Little, Brown and Company (UK)
Brettenham House
Lancaster Place
London WC2E 7EN

CONTENTS

INTRODUCTION

Belinda

When I started painting furniture in the early 1970s as a hobby, it was as a result of being lent two very different American books on the subject within a week of each other. These inspired me to such an extent that I was determined to try my hand at it. For a Mum with two small children, furniture painting was the ideal pastime, giving me huge creative satisfaction when there was time between the fish fingers, school runs and ironing, and also giving lasting pleasure to others – initially to my children, and later to friends and clients who brought their shabby pieces to me for rejuvenation. A toy box which I clothed in blue with white painted lace and pink roses for my daughter, then four years old, still nestles at the end of her bed, its now grown-up owner refusing all offers of a re-paint!

The immense pleasure I derived from those early painting days lives with me still, but I had no idea then how popular this art was to become or how radically it would change over the next two decades, both in style and in the materials used. In the 1960s and early 70s, white gloss was the standard choice for anything painted, but in time beautifully coloured things began to appear in the shops. Most

were designed with children in mind, but childhood lasts for such a short time – I felt that grown-ups should also be able to enjoy painted furniture.

Researching into designs in the folk traditions of Scandinavia and of Austria, Germany and Switzerland, the forerunners of what we know today as Pennsylvanian Dutch (derived from the German *Deutsch*), I was inspired by their dower chests and wardrobes, with backgrounds painted in deep blues or reds, and panels overflowing with disciplined squirls and flowers. I became a 'doodler', sketching ideas based on designs two to three centuries old. Much of the painting was charmingly primitive, every element stylized to make it simpler to execute, but the pleasure enjoyed by the unknown artists in their craft shines through the paint to this day.

In the 1970s, only oil-based paints were deemed suitable for furniture, and the neccessary primer, undercoat and two top coats took at least four days to complete, and preferably longer to cure. I would start on a piece, my mind brimming over with a vision of the finished object, only to find that my enthusiasm had somewhat waned by the time it was ready for the design to be painted. Then came the frustration of acrylic tube paints not sticking properly to the oil-based surface. The discovery was not usually made until the design had been carefully drawn on the item, after which I would have to remove it to key the eggshell paint before re-drawing. So many pitfalls! Since the fashion then was for flat colours with no finishes, all blemishes such as cracks had to be filled and laboriously sanded. From start to finish, the process was slow by today's standards.

Gradually, over the last decade, taste has changed to a nostalgic yearning for the old and even shabby distressed look – a blissful style, very easy to live with, and much easier and quicker to paint! It almost obviates the need for filling cracks and holes, as blemishes help to create the 'old' look and we don't have to worry too much if perchance it chips later. It even necessitates the use of the quicker-drying water-based paints, as they can give a more realistic distressed look than their slow-drying oil-based equivalents, making it possible to paint in a matter of days a piece that would once have taken at least two weeks.

Another change was a new fashion for 'finishes', a broken coat of coloured glaze rather than flat paint, both on walls and furniture. Dozens of books have been written on various finishes, including several on painting furniture. If you collect them, you will realize that they are very similar to cookery books! There is a treasured recipe or two in every one, but each of us finds, after much experimentation, our favourite recipe for a particular finish or look.

The pleasure and satisfaction I derived from turning unlovely objects into treasurable pieces in those early years was like being given the most wonderful present, one I felt too good not to share with others. One dream was to have a school devoted to painting furniture where anyone could come for a day or a week to learn the possibilities and, most of all, be inspired; the second dream, of course, was to write a book! The first dream came true in 1991, when I opened my school in Malmesbury. We have welcomed people from all over the world, and one of the questions they often ask is 'When are you going to write a book?'. Well, that time has come, and my second dream has now come true!

When I came to plan it, so many ideas flooded in that they would easily have filled several volumes. After much honing, I have tried to include examples of many different techniques, so hopefully there is something to appeal to all tastes. Strangely, the more I experiment with mixtures and new ideas, the

more I find that the simplest ones are usually the most effective. Many of the finishes shown here, such as marbleizing, can be achieved with either oil- or water-based products, as can the final varnishing, but with the growing awareness of how fragile our environment is, many new solvent-free products are appearing on the market. Keeping up with the newest paint and varnish technology is quite difficult, but I am sure that within a few years the oil-based products which we are so used to will die out, being replaced by better and more durable water-based ones.

As for the design work, which is my first love, we are not all lucky enough to have the confidence to attempt freehand designs without being daunted. For this reason, the book includes tracings and stencils. Because I am lucky enough to have been able to enjoy freehand painting from the beginning, I am guilty of having neglected stencilling until the idea came to me of using stencils as guides in conjunction with freehand washes, which gives security yet offers the option of your own freehand expression.

When painting a design on a dark base coat, the colours need the addition of white paint to make them show; unfortunately, this causes the colours to become opaque, which one does not necessarily want. If the design is carried out first in white paint and the colours are then laid over it, however, they remain clear, and the light shines through. Why not, I thought, use the same method by stencilling first in white? The results were very pleasing, as I hope you will discover.

On researching into the historical use of stencils, I found that originally they evolved as an aid for the decorative artist. As long ago as the first century BC they were used to adorn Chinese temple walls with patterns

and sacred texts; later, in the middle ages, Scandinavian church ceilings were spangled with stencilled stars and borders before the rest of the design was added by hand. The very word 'stencil', derives from the Latin *stincilla* meaning a spark; from thence to the Old French for 'to sparkle or cover with stars' – *estenciller*. So the original stencil was a simple star-shaped tool, cut from anything durable enough, to aid repetition. (In Fiji, ancient banana-skin stencils have been found!)

The urge to decorate and beautify our surroundings has been with us since time immemorial, starting as far back as the primitive wall paintings of pre-historic times. Over 3,000 years ago the ancient Egyptians discovered a perfect way to paint furniture, not dissimilar to the much later use of gesso, by giving a piece a thin coat of adhesive plaster, smoothing it and applying pigments. The Egyptians have probably had the greatest influence on painted furniture as well as style through thousands of years, their tombs originally being raided by the Greeks, who in turn influenced the Romans.

But let us come forward in time to the earliest painted furniture as we know it today, which appeared in Norway at the end of the sixteenth century. It seems that we have two parallels in furniture painting: first, the provincial style, which stems from a folk art tradition the roots of which lie in the mists of time, carried out by rural communities all over Western and Eastern Europe; the second, which was developed to please the nobility, and was influenced by travel, trade and fashion.

From the early middle ages until the sixteenth century, most European decoration had been carved rather than painted, decorative painting being mainly restricted to walls and ceilings. (At that time,

Pompeii was still hidden under the ash from Vesuvius and the Egyptian tombs had not been re-discovered!)

By the beginning of the seventeenth century, the desire to decorate everyday objects arose all over rural Europe and Scandinavia, the designs being similar to or to blend with those of the familiar wood carvings. Most of the sparse furnishings of those days were large simple pieces, such as cupboards and chests, generally made of inexpensive woods, with no preservative to prevent damp or insect damage. The logical solution was to protect them with paint, which also offered the pleasure of something beautiful and cheerful in the home, often commemorating a celebration such as a wedding.

This folk style of painting continued for over 200 years, influenced only a little by the changing styles of fashion. Meanwhile, the ever-fighting courts of Europe gained artistic influence as well as lands from their wars. The Italian Renaissance spread to France via Francis I, who employed Italian artists to decorate his palace at Fontainbleau. The great decorative age of the Baroque had begun, its influence spreading to Austria, Germany, Switzerland, Russia and also Scandinavia, where the Cs and Ss of Norwegian Rosemaling imitated the curling fronds of the carved and printed acanthus leaf so much used in Renaissance Italy.

By 1650, the Sun King, Louis X1V, was on the throne of France. His palace at Versailles is still a monument to the Baroque style of decoration. In its wonderfully over-ornate and sumptuous rooms, much of the furniture was made of pine, this inferior wood being coated in gesso and painted, with much accompanying gilding.

Trade with the East was increasing. Finely-painted porcelain and silk had been the main imports during most of the seventeenth century, then the first pieces of Chinese lacquered furniture began to arrive, captivating the nobility in France and, by 1680, courts all over Europe. Chinoiserie became one of the most longlasting fashions, influencing not only the courts of Europe but folk painters such as those of Hinderloopen in Holland.

By the mid-1700s, almost every royal palace had a Chinese room or pavilion. Cabinetmakers sought to recreate the incredibly popular lacquer furniture by developing ways of imitating it. In England, during Queen Anne's productive reign, many beautiful red and black 'lacquer' pieces were produced. The technique was especially popular in Italy, where the cabinetmakers' skills were deteriorating, and faulty craftsmanship was disguised with painted gesso. In France, the brothers Martin invented their vernis Martin, producing a translucent finish very similar to and possibly surpassing true lacquer.

During the eighteenth century the strong Baroque style softened into the Rococo. There were still swirling acanthus leaves, but rampant gilding gave way to softer polychrome colours. In a desire to create surroundings which were more cosy and less grand, lighter and more portable furniture was designed to fit smaller rooms, and was painted in paler matching colours, to blend with painted panelling or brocade upholstery. Grisailles, a style of painting in various shades of grey to imitate relief carving in stone, became popular. Paintings of romantic nymphs and shepherds in wooded settings with waterfalls and grottoes adorned walls and larger furniture, the rocks of the latter

BELOW. This coffer, typical of the Tyrolean provincial style, was painted in 1800. The flower borders, panels and the apron, on which the date is painted, all employ the use of the curved brushstroke (see tear-shaped leaves, page 43). Apart from the detailed panels with figures, the design would not be difficult to reproduce.

giving Rococo its name.

Delicate subtle colours were the hallmark of the Rococo style in Sweden, where a Chinese pavilion was created for the Queen at Drottning-holm Castle. The romantic style in Sweden was fairly short-lived, however, the less-than-frivolous Gustavus III seizing power in 1771.

This occurred soon after the discovery of the ruins of Pompeii and Herculanum, which opened a new and exciting chapter in the style of interiors and painted furniture. Italy once again influenced the change, when it was visited by the architect Robert Adam. He was enraptured by the classic shapes of temples and columns, so much so that he persuaded artists including Zucci, Angelica Kauffmann, and Piranesi, who had done wonderful drawings of the ruins, to come to England to help him with his idea, which was for the first time to create houses with interiors that would reflect their exteriors. This was the beginning of Neoclassicism. Interiors were richly painted with a classical theme, the furniture for the first time being specially designed and painted to be in keeping with its surroundings.

The fashion reached Sweden, where King Gustavus gave his name to what has become known as the Gustavian style. The lines of furniture were similar, but colours were quieter and more sombre. Nowadays we look at those colours and envy their serenity.

The Neoclassical influence and the enduring fascination for Chinoiserie reached new heights soon afterwards with Mr Chippendale's designs for furniture, much of which was painted. His, and later Sheraton's, pattern books were published in French and Italian as well as English, and soon reached not only Europe, but also America. Here, the emigrants that had arrived fifty years earlier had

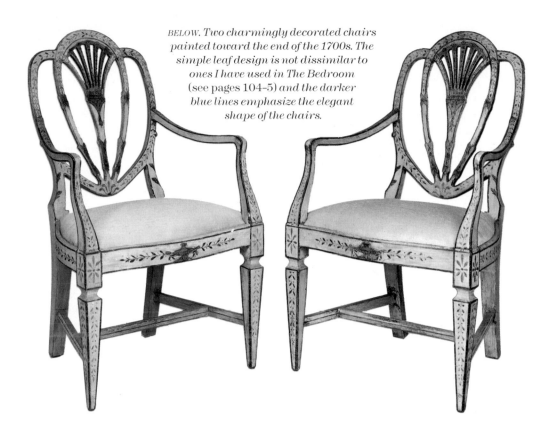

BELOW. Two charmingly decorated chairs painted toward the end of the 1700s. The simple leaf design is not dissimilar to ones I have used in The Bedroom (see pages 104–5) and the darker blue lines emphasize the elegant shape of the chairs.

brought with them vivid memories of their styles of folk painting, which were gradually re-interpreted as materials and demand grew in their new country.

The influence of Messrs Chippendale and Sheraton on style and painting was enormous, not only encouraging the complete painting of a piece, but also introducing the delicacy of painting on satinwood, one of the most elegant and beautiful forms of painted furniture.

With Napoleon came the Empire style. The classic influence was still very much present, but more ornate, regal, and verging on the pompous, much painted carving and gilding re-appearing on furniture. A few years later, the Prince Regent embarked upon the creation of the Royal Pavilion in Brighton – a fantasy mixture of Chinoiserie, colour, and sheer whimsy, with painted furniture to match. At about the same time, the Empire style reached America, where furniture makers imitated the

gilding on furniture with stencils, using gold or bronze powders and shading them to resemble trompe l'oeil carving (or relief). By 1820, a Mr Hancock, seeing the possibilities of stencilling, started a factory producing stencilled chairs. These were immensely popular and heralded the advent of mass-produced furniture.

The fashion for painted furniture has re-emerged from time to time since the end of the nineteenth century, but has not lasted for long until recently. It is mainly the rustic furniture that has regained popularity, but more companies are making things specially to be painted, so maybe we shall see a new golden age of elegance, taking our inspiration from past styles or developing a new one of our own. Whatever your taste, I hope that you will find the same endless pleasure that I do in experimenting with some of the decorative and paint techniques demonstrated in this book.

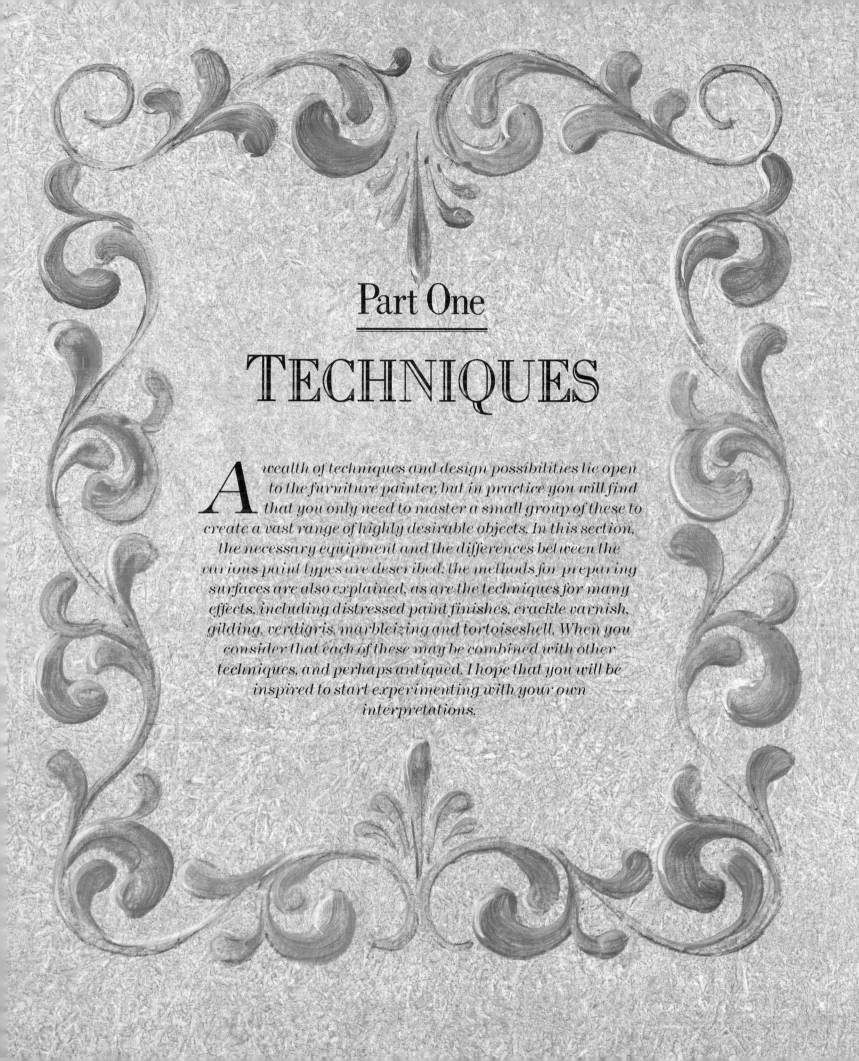

Part One

TECHNIQUES

A wealth of techniques and design possibilities lie open to the furniture painter, but in practice you will find that you only need to master a small group of these to create a vast range of highly desirable objects. In this section, the necessary equipment and the differences between the various paint types are described; the methods for preparing surfaces are also explained, as are the techniques for many effects, including distressed paint finishes, crackle varnish, gilding, verdigris, marbleizing and tortoiseshell. When you consider that each of these may be combined with other techniques, and perhaps antiqued, I hope that you will be inspired to start experimenting with your own interpretations.

MATERIALS AND EQUIPMENT

Given the choice between shopping for clothes or for paint and brushes, for me, there is no contest, the latter wins every time! The glee with which I bring home a new pot of paint or a pristine varnish brush and try them out for the first time knows no bounds. A fortune could be spent on such things, but there is no need to do so – it's far better to start with a few basic essentials and add to the collection only as and when other materials or equipment become necessary.

Much of the equipment we use can be found around the home; this includes old jam jars, aluminium take-away trays, plastic carrier bags and old newspapers. Two or three brushes for base coats and varnishing should suffice to start with; the more brushes you have, the more you use, so an added advantage of only having a few brushes is that they are likely to be cleaned more regularly than a wider range! The materials we will be using can loosely be divided into four 'families', summarized in the chart on page 14.

All paint is made by mixing coloured pigments into a liquid, and binding them with something to make them stick together. The four paint families are categorized according to whether the liquid and binder are based on oil, water, cellulose or methylated spirits. Within each of the four families, there are dozens of products; each of these can be mixed with other paints within the same family. Occasionally, it is possible to mix certain paints from the different families.

THE OIL-BASED FAMILY

So called since the pigments are ground together with oils such as linseed, this is the group with which we are probably most familiar, and includes primer, undercoat, and gloss or satin finish paint for woodwork. Runny or non-drip, oil paints take several hours or overnight to dry. The brushes must be cleaned in a solvent, which may be either white spirit or turpentine; when the paint is dry, the only solvent is paint stripper.

Varnishes, such as yacht varnish or polyurethane varnish, are also oil based, but some water-based varnishes now contain polyurethane, so always read the tin carefully to check in which group a varnish belongs.

Ready-made oil glaze and the thicker scumble glaze are available in tins; some are tinted and some are more or less colourless, which allows you to add your own tints. Varnishes and glazes in the oil family tend to be a little yellow, and can become increasingly so with age, both on furniture or when left in the tin.

All the above can be mixed with each other if need be, and all can be tinted with oil-tube paint, whether artists', students' or alkyds.

Also in this family is 3-hour goldsize, an oil-based glue used in gilding for sticking on leaf. This can also be used on its own, either as a varnish or as the first coat of the two needed to achieve a crackled varnish or 'cracklure' (*see pages 34*).

Because all oil-based paints and varnishes are slow drying, they have time to level themselves after application and are thus less likely to show brush-marks than their water-based counterparts. To slow the drying time still more if need be, add a little linseed oil. To speed it up, add a little Terebine. To thin oil-based paints, and to clean brushes, use white spirit.

Oil-based 'cousins' include enamels, such as those used for model making, Japan colours and even waxes, such as furniture or shoe polish. Waxes cannot be mixed with tinned paint or varnish, but if a wax is soft enough it can be coloured by mixing it with oil-tube paint or powder pigments.

THE WATER-BASED FAMILY

As all the members of this family are water soluble, brushes can be cleaned in water.

On its own, a pigment suspended in water would not stick to a surface once the water had evaporated, so various 'binders' are used. A chemically-made PVA or acrylic is the commonest type of binder for emulsions and varnishes, both of which are waterproof when dry. Not so waterproof are the softer paints, such as distemper, gesso and casein paint, bound by rabbit skin size or casein, an extract of milk.

Another non-waterproof binder, used in watercolours and gouache, is liquid gum arabic. This is also used for the second coat of a crackle varnish (*see page 34*), and can be applied over a water- or spirit-based surface to make the subsequent coat of water-based paint crack.

All water-based paints, glazes and varnishes dry quickly in comparison to their oil-based equivalents, taking from half an hour upwards, and they do not yellow with age. It is more difficult to obliterate brush marks, but this can be turned to our advantage for some finishes. When varnishing, try to use a brush with nylon or manmade bristles, which leave fewer marks than real bristle.

The solvent for all waterproof members of the family, when dry, is methylated spirit. For non-waterproof ones, it is water.

Acrylic scumble glaze, used for effects such as marbling, does not remain workable for as long as the oil-based scumble, so a smaller area

1 Hog hair duster: *for softening or stipple effects*
2 Badger softener: *for blending glazes*
3 Decorator's brush: *available in various sizes*
4 Flat fibre brush: *for use with bleach*
5 Bristle varnish brush: *available in various sizes*
6 Bristle varnish brush (trimmed): *for use with Polyfilla for textures*
7 Soft hair brush: *for varnishes or smoothing leaf*
8 Stencil brush: *available in various sizes*
9 Hog hair square fitch: *for general use*
10 Hog hair filbert fitch: *for applying waxes and bronze powder stencilling*
11 Flat nylon brush: *for water-based and acrylic varnishes and paints*
12 Long coachlining brush: *for long straight lines*
13 Short coachlining brush: *for curved lines*
14, 15 and 16 Design brushes: *in different sizes*

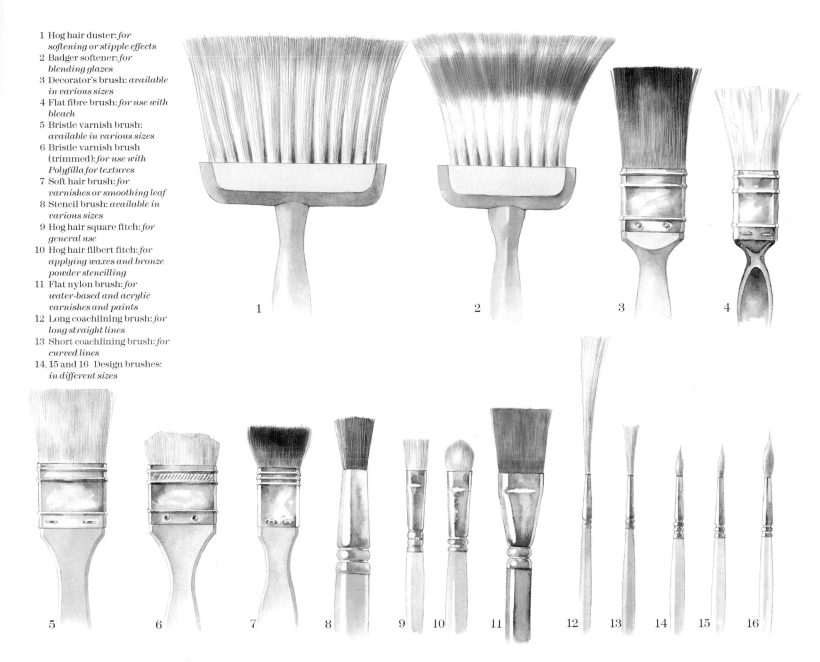

should be completed at a time, with subsequent areas overlapping slightly.

There are many acrylic varnishes and mediums, ranging from tough varnishes for floors to artists' mediums, which are designed to be mixed with acrylic tube paints or used over them. All are similar but of differing thicknesses, and all can be tinted with emulsion, acrylic or gouache tube paints, the latter being rendered waterproof by the mixture. Some acrylic varnishes are not as strong as the oil-based types, but some makes will adhere to an oil-based surface, and even to glass, porcelain or metal.

Where it is possible to speed up the drying time of oils, for this family there are retarders, which can slow the drying time when necessary.

Other intermixable cousins in the family are white water-based glues, such as Unibond and PVA wood glues, and wallpaper sealer. These vary in strength and can be used, diluted with water, as a priming or keying coat on metal, enamel or porcelain. Beware of non-waterproof glues as they act very like liquid gum arabic, causing any subsequent water-based coat to crack.

There are also water-based 'goldsizes' for gilding which remain tacky and usable for at least thirty-six hours.

THE METHYLATED SPIRIT FAMILY

This family contains dozens of products, but we only need to think about a few. The solvent for this family is methylated spirit (or alcohol). The other main constituent is 'shellac' – a deposit left on the branches of several species of Asian trees by insects which have fed on the sap.

Shellac flakes, which are orange/brown in colour, are dissolved in methylated spirit to form a very useful sealer/lacquer. This is compatible with all the other families, and can be used as a primer to seal wood or a painted surface, as a barrier between different coats, or over paint to 'antique' it. As shellac dries quite quickly, it is difficult to apply an even coat, so always use it sparingly and try not to go back over parts that are already drying.

Other members of the family are sanding sealer or patent knotting, both of which are a lighter colour and are normally used to seal wood and prevent sap seeping from knots. French polish is made from shellac; an easier, brushable version, used for penwork (*see pages 48 and 68–72*), is white polish. All of these are meths-soluble even when dry, so when using more than one coat it is necessary to work as quickly as possible, to avoid affecting the previous coat.

THE CELLULOSE-BASED FAMILY
Cellulose is the sort of paint that is used on cars and can be bought in spray cans. These paints are not as durable as those in the last three families and may yellow with age. They will crack and peel off if used over an oil-based surface, so only use them over paints from the other families. Even glossy cellulose surfaces will accept water-based glazes or a design in acrylics over them, to be sealed with oil- or water-based varnish.

Similar to these is the type of paint specially formulated for metal. This needs no primer or undercoat, one or two coats covering well. A drawback is that one needs specially-formulated solvent or thinners for cleaning brushes; the solvent is quite expensive and evaporates easily, so it is probably cheaper to buy a very inexpensive brush, and throw it away after use.

TABLE OF PAINT FAMILIES

TYPE	OIL-BASED	WATER-BASED	METHS-BASED	CELLULOSE-BASED
Primers	White, pink, red oxide, aluminium	Acrylic primer/undercoat, Unibond + water	Sanding sealer, patent knotting, shellac, button polish	Car spray primer
Undercoats	Small range of colours – matt	Second coat of acrylic primer/undercoat, or coat of emulsion	—	—
Top coats	Flat (matt), satin or eggshell (mid-sheen), gloss, enamel, spray cans	Waterproof: matt emulsion, silk vinyl (mid-sheen), acrylic eggshell Porous: distemper, gesso, casein paint, Plaka	—	Matt, satin & gloss sprays, tins of metal paint
Stains	Oil-based wood stains	Emulsion + 4-5 parts water, acrylic tube paint + water	—	—
Glazes	Transparent oil or scumble	Acrylic scumble	—	—
Glues	3-hour goldsize	Waterproof: water-based goldsize, Unibond, PVA wood glue Non-waterproof: liquid gum arabic	—	—
Varnishes	Matt, satin or gloss, yacht varnish, tinted 'woodtones'	Matt, satin or gloss; internal external & for floors	—	—
Lacquers	—	(Varnish is sometimes called lacquer)	Sanding sealer, shellac, white polish, button polish, transparent lacquer	Cellulose lacquer
Waxes	Stain waxes in wood colours, white wax, liming wax, furniture wax	Acrylic wax	—	—
Sealer for wax	—	—	White polish	—
Antiquing agents	Oil-tube paint + white spirit, tinted varnish or glaze	Acrylic scumble or varnish + acrylic tube paint, or stains	Shellac or shellac + sanding sealer	—
Liming	Liming wax	Liming paste	—	—
Verdigris	Liming wax + oil-tube paint	Liming paste + designers' gouache	—	—
Tinters/colourants	Oil-tube paints, artists', students' or alkyd, universal stainers, powder pigments	Acrylic tube paints, designers' gouache, universal stainers, powder pigments mixed with a little water	Spirit stains, aniline spirit dyes	Oil-tube paint mixed with a little white spirit for metal paints
Solvent/thinner	White spirit or turps	Water	Methylated spirit	Cellulose thinners
Solvents when dry	Paint stripper	Methylated spirit	Methylated spirit	—
Characteristics				
Drying time	6-72 hours	$\frac{1}{2}$-24 hours	$\frac{1}{2}$-$\frac{3}{4}$ hour, more for subsequent coats	$\frac{1}{2}$-$\frac{3}{4}$ hour
Curing time	2 weeks	3-4 days	2-3 hours	5-6 weeks for maximum cure
Compatability	Will go over all other 'families'	Will go over meths- & cellulose-based & some brands over oil-based	Will go over all other 'families', long-term adhesion to oil-based not certain	Will go over water- or meths-based. Peels if put over oil-based

PREPARING SURFACES

We tend to think that if we wish to paint something old, it must be completely stripped; or to paint over new wood, it must first be sealed and primed. This is not necessarily so. How you prepare anything depends entirely on how you want it to look when it is finished. So start by choosing the finish you want before you reach for the sandpaper, primer and elbow grease; by thinking from the end product backwards, you can save a lot of time and energy. The most important factor is that the new paint should either stick when you want it to, or not too well if you want to distress it. Old gloss paint does not necessarily have to be removed, and new wood does not always have to be primed with paint (certainly not if you want a distressed paint finish with the wood showing through). By taking you through lots of different possibilities, I hope to be able to save you some time and energy. Of course fairly laborious preparation is sometimes needed, but if, like me, you have a constant desire to find short cuts, there are many lovely effects which are much quicker and easier to prepare than you might imagine.

KEYING THE SURFACE

Whatever the surface of the piece, if it has handles the first job is to remove them if possible, as painting round them is fiddly. They can then be cleaned, if necessary, or replaced with new ones, which can often improve the whole piece. If you are fitting new ones, the old holes may need to be filled.

Let us start with old brown shiny furniture – sideboards and chests of drawers of the 1940s and 1950s. Whichever finish you choose, the shine has to go – so simply rub all over, by hand or with an electric sander. Go with the grain and use medium-to-coarse sandpaper to 'key' the surface. Even with a sander you will probably still need to rub indentations and mouldings by hand. The amount of keying depends on whether you want a distressed finish, revealing the wood through the paint, or want the wood to be completely covered.

For a distressed effect, the sanding can be a little less comprehensive than for a complete repaint. For the former, sand and then paint one coat of emulsion; in general, try to use a medium-to-dark tone for darker woods to avoid too much contrast.

For a completely painted surface, sand and coat with acrylic primer/undercoat, or for a really durable surface, use oil-based primer (the strongest is aluminium primer).

After an acrylic primer/undercoat, either water-based emulsion can be used or oil-based flat, undercoat, satin or gloss paint. After oil-based primers, it is advisable to use only oil-based paints, as water does not readily cling to oil. Even if it does adhere, it may be prone to chipping later.

After sanding and priming with acrylic primer/undercoat, the old stain on brown furniture can sometimes seep into the new coat, discolouring it. If this happens, go over the surface with shellac or sanding sealer, repeating the primer when this has dried.

If you wish to lighten the wood colour, use wood bleach from a decorators' merchant; do this after removing every bit of the previous finish, right back to the bare wood, and before doing anything else.

PAINTED FURNITURE

If pine furniture is varnished, you can simply rub it with medium sandpaper to key the surface. Many of us, however, possess furniture that has already been painted, usually with white gloss paint. This can of course be stripped by dipping or using a paint stripper, following the manufacturer's instructions, but if you don't want to go to these lengths, it is usually possible to paint over the existing paint, providing there are no ugly old paint runs. Chips do not matter too much, in fact they can be turned to advantage if the piece is ultimately to be antiqued, the dents and blemishes giving it a more realistic aged effect (see the chair on page 106 and glass-fronted cupboard on page 75).

First, the old paint must be keyed: rub thoroughly, following the direction of the grain and using medium sandpaper, and remove any loose paint. Any chips through which the wood can be seen should be patched with acrylic primer/undercoat.

Now there are two choices: either coat the surface completely with an acrylic primer/undercoat and continue with oil- or water-based paints and/or glazes, or, very sparingly, drag straight over the old surface with oil-based paint. To do this, pull the paint out, still working along the grain, so that it gives a streaky, dragged look, with the old gloss paint underneath just showing through.

WAXED SURFACES

If you are painting old pine, or any wood that has been waxed over the years, the most important thing is to remove the wax, as no paint will readily adhere to it. For this, we need to use a wax solvent; white spirit, meths, chemical brush cleanser or liquid stripper will do, and even some kitchen cleaners. (If they 'cut through the grease', they may also 'cut through the wax'!)

Start with the mildest solvents – white spirit or meths – only resorting to the others if it becomes essential. Put some of the solvent on fine wire wool, smear it over the surface of the wood and let it soak in a little to dissolve the wax. Re-wet the wire wool and rub it along the grain. This is where old-fashioned elbow grease comes in. After a while the wax should begin to appear on the wire wool. Replace the used wool with a new piece periodically, when the former becomes covered with wax. Keep wetting and rubbing until the surface feels wax-free when you run your fingers over it. Wipe with warm soapy water and continue as follows.

Use one coat of emulsion for distressing back to the wood; with pale woods such as pine, try to use a medium-to-light tone, as darker colours give too great a contrast when distressed over light wood. For a completely painted look, use acrylic primer/undercoat or an oil-based primer, such as aluminium primer. The latter must be followed only by oil-based paint, the former may be followed by either oil- or water-based paint.

NEW WOOD

Brand new, unfinished woods, such as pine, oak or mahogany, do not need to be sanded before you start to apply your chosen effect. The first option is to bleach them, using special wood bleach from a decorators' merchant and following the manufacturer's instructions. After this, they can either be stained or painted.

To stain, either use a ready-made wood stain, or emulsion mixed with 4–5 parts of water, or even acrylic tube paint diluted with water. Seal the stain in with either sanding sealer, water-based varnish or a PVA waterproof glue diluted with water so that it is thin enough to paint with.

For a distressed paint finish, first seal the new wood with shellac, which will deepen the colour, or with sanding sealer, which will not. Then apply just

one coat of emulsion or white acrylic primer/undercoat, which is very similar to it, distressing it when dry (*see pages 18–21*).

For an even more distressed look, new wood can be physically distressed before it is sealed with shellac. There are various tools one can use, the easiest is a stone – flint for preference. Press this into the wood in places where it would be logical to expect damage, such as the edges, turning the stone so the dents are different shapes; there is no need to bang hard as new pine is very soft and dents easily.

This can be taken a step further by adding wood worm holes! Using an awl, held upright like a dagger, sprinkle a small area of the surface with little holes, varying the pressure to give different sizes. Worm 'runs' can also be very effective: hold the awl at an angle of about thirty degrees to the surface, rather as you would hold a knife; press the tip into the lighter-coloured soft grain and, still pressing, draw it towards you, denting the soft grain. After a centimetre or so, angle the awl to right or left and draw it over the neighbouring, darker hard grain and into the next soft grain, then press along that for another centimetre before crossing back to the original light grain.

If you are giving new wood a complete paint finish, it must first be primed. Use acrylic primer/undercoat or an oil-based primer. When dry, any cracks or holes can be filled with wood filler, then the whole surface should be rubbed smooth with medium-to-fine sandpaper. The former can be followed by either oil- or water-based paint, the latter only by oil-based. If you intend to put a glaze finish on top, it is wise to apply at least two coats of oil-based mid-sheen paint, or silk vinyl, lightly sanding between them to create a really smooth surface for the glaze.

METAL SURFACES

If your surface is metal, whether aluminium, tin or enamel, the water-

based paints are not strong enough to be durable because the ridgidity of the metal can cause chips if the painted surface is knocked. Some very good cellulose-based paints have been developed for metal, or you can use old-fashioned oil-based enamels, or even car spray paints – though the latter should be used carefully and infrequently for the sake of our poor ozone layer! If the metal object is old and rusty, remove as much rust as possible with a wire brush. Rust preventers are available for very bad surfaces, but these are not normally required.

After this, we have two possibilities. Either apply a coat of metal primer, which is oil-based, followed by an oil-based undercoat and two oil-based top coats or, alternatively, use one or two coats of cellulose metal paint. If the surface is reasonably sound, the cellulose metal paint will suffice, and you will not need a primer.

Cellulose metal paint and car spray paint are compatible with water-based paints, so a finish or design using acrylic paints or glaze can be applied over them.

If you have used oil-based paints, you will be able to continue with acrylics after either giving the dry, painted base coat a coat of shellac or sanding sealer, or wiping it with a damp sponge dipped in fullers' earth.

TILES AND OTHER PORCELAIN SURFACES

Porcelain surfaces, such as tiles, cannot be keyed by rubbing down, even with wet-and-dry paper. Instead, you will need to coat them with a keying solution. For the bathroom on *page 108*, we used Unibond glue diluted with about two parts of water. This was painted all over and allowed to dry.

There are also special oil-based primers for tiles; these need several days to dry. Always remember that all paints, glazes and varnishes, whether water- or oil-based, need time to dry hard or 'cure', and even when they feel touch-dry they still need more time to reach maximum durability; this is roughly from three to four days for water-based products, and fourteen or more for oil-based ones. These curing times increase with the number of coats applied.

Before starting on a tile project, try out the available products on some loose tiles, then give them the nail test! Scratch the surface with your nail after the appropriate curing time – if the coating comes off, it's not strong enough. After oil-based primer, oil-based paint must be used; after the glue, you can use either oil- or water-based paints. If it is ultimately varnished with several coats of durable oil- or water-based varnish, an ordinary emulsion on top of the glue should be strong enough, provided it is gently cleaned with liquid rather than an abrasive cleaner.

Special paints are available if you want to put a design directly onto a ceramic surface: the water-based types need to be put in the oven for a short time after painting; the oil-based varieties need no firing, but they should be sealed with their own oil-based varnish.

FORMICA AND MELAMINE

There are other surfaces, of the types commonly found in kitchens, such as Formica and Melamine, which are not so easy to key. Some have a satin finish, while others are very shiny. The satin ones will accept oil- or water-based scumble glaze, even without sanding, and provided the scumble finish is thoroughly varnished when dry, it should be pretty durable. The really shiny ones need a good rub with medium wet-and-dry paper, moistened with water to make it grip. Even then, paint may not adhere well, so give the surface a coat of waterproof white PVA glue diluted with water to make it paintable. Follow this with oil- or water-based paint and/or glaze, sealing again with at least two coats of oil-based varnish or three or four of

water-based, allowing whichever you use time to cure, so the coats reach their maximum hardness.

PLASTIC

Plastic, such as the urn on *page 99* and the flowerpot on *page 116*, is prone to bend, so it needs a key which will bend with it. Again, the surface can be keyed with a water-based sealer, such as waterproof white glue, diluted with water and allowed to dry thoroughly; this will remain bendable and accept subsequent coats of water-based paint, forming a cushion so that the paint will dent rather than chip if knocked. Always seal with two or three coats of water-based acrylic varnish to complete the cushion – oil-based varnish dries to a more brittle finish.

TERRACOTTA AND PLASTER

Terracotta and plaster are both porous, so to achieve a solid paint finish you must seal them either with water-based varnish, with glue, as above, or with sanding sealer or shellac. This can be followed by an oil- or water-based paint, and then finished with an appropriate varnish.

Before sealing, terracotta or plaster can be treated like new wood with a stain or wash of watery colour, then sealed as above and varnished. If you are painting a terracotta pot which is to be used to hold plants, the moisture from the earth will seep through the terracotta and could damage the outer paint effect unless you take the precaution of sealing, painting and varnishing the inside as well as the outer surface.

After sealing, instead of varnishing, they can be limed as for wood (*see page 99*), using a plain white or tinted liming wax or paste, depending on the end use. Indoors, the wax should provide adequate protection for decorative items; for outside or anywhere where washing down or cleaning may be necessary, use the paste and then varnish with oil-based varnish (*see the chair on page 98 and planter on page 99*).

FABRICS

Fabrics are different again. In most cases, it is advisable to first wash your fabric in order to remove any dressing, but this not always necessary, so check the paint manufacturer's instructions before you begin. The various paints that have been designed for fabrics include some that are suitable for painting on natural fibres, such as silks and cottons, as well as others, specifically certain types of transfer paints and crayons, that are designed for use with synthetics, such as nylon. To use the transfer type, you must first draw or paint the design on paper, and then iron it on the fabric, rather like an old-fashioned embroidery transfer.

The silk fabric paints are available in a wide range of beautiful colours, all of which can be blended on the fabric like watercolours. Some of our trace-ons could be used on silk; using dressmaker's carbon paper, carefully trace the design on the fabric, then go over the traced lines with gutta percha, which is a tree gum long used for this purpose in the Far East. (Applicators rather like pens, producing a very thin line, can be purchased from specialist craft suppliers.) The resin outlines will act as barriers to prevent the silk paints seeping from one area to another, thus giving you the freedom to blend colours as you go with no danger of blurred outlines.

Other fabric paints are opaque, giving a more solid effect, as are the paints specially formulated for stencilling on fabric. Fabric paints designed for one type of fibre may still work on other types, though the colours may not be so strong, so it is worth experimenting.

Most of these paints need to be ironed after they have dried, to make them durable. Whatever you use, follow the manufacturer's instructions. For a painted blind, stiffen the fabric first with a spray stiffener, then paint or stencil and iron. For cushions or bedspreads, choose a thickish, closely-woven fabric, such as calico (*see pages 96 and 98*).

PAINT FINISHES

There are hundreds of different paint effects, and in general the most attractive of these are very easy to create. Some are achieved through many coats of this and that, with exhaustive sanding between each; very beautiful they may be, but I have a low boredom threshold, and no masochistic streak whatsoever, so I aim to achieve stunning finishes in the quickest and simplest ways possible.

The choice of finish rather depends on the nature of the existing surface; for instance, if the item is an old white gloss cupboard, it would be inappropriate to aim for a 'distressed' look with the wood showing through, as you would have to expend huge amounts of sandpaper and energy unless the piece was first stripped. The sensible choice would be a finish that would cover the existing paint, saving much time and mess or expense. If a surface is badly chipped and cracked, turn this to advantage by re-painting over the damaged surface and 'antiquing' so that the little blemishes contribute to the aged effect, rather than attempting marbleizing or tortoiseshell, which call for an absolutely smooth surface.

DISTRESSING

Let us start with the finishes where paint is put on and then removed again, called 'distressing'. There are two ways to distress paint: physically, with abrasives such as sandpaper or wet-and-dry paper, or chemically by using solvents, such as turpentine, white spirit or methylated spirit.

For the simplest of all distressed paint, over old or new wood, the piece must first be appropriately prepared (*see pages 15–17*). Next, it is given one coat of emulsion undiluted from the tin; always smooth the brush strokes with the grain of the wood, making sure it is not too thick and that there are no runs (it is always a good idea to check for these before rinsing the brush – they seem to appear, especially on chairs, however careful one is). When the emulsion is dry, usually after about half an hour, take some medium sandpaper and, using it like a rasp, scuff the paint from certain places, going with the grain.

Start with any right-angles or sharpish edges, imagining where the piece would have taken wear and tear over the years: on doors and drawers, rub round the handles and where hands would have pushed them shut; on chairs, where feet would have worn the rails and boots would have bumped the legs; where hands clutch arms day after day and buttons rub on the backs, also the edge of the seat and maybe the seat itself. Don't distress too heavily to start with; work gently and then stand back for an overall look, adding a little or emphasizing here and there until you are happy and convinced by the effect. On larger areas, such as tops and sides of chests or dressers, distress random patches in areas likely to suffer wear and tear, always going with the grain.

Next, you have several options. If you want a design, this is the time to apply it. You might give the piece a coat of water-based satin varnish first; this will act as a barrier in case the design goes wrong, making it easier to wipe off. Alternatively, apply a streaky coat of shellac over the distressed emulsion, always going in the same direction as the original brushmarks.

SIMPLE DISTRESSED

1 Having keyed the surface with medium sandpaper, apply one coat of emulsion (here, blue emulsion on oak), the brushmarks going with the grain of the wood; when dry, the paint will be distressed in places.

2 Remove the paint in places with medium sandpaper or wet-and-dry paper, rubbing with the grain to create streaks. Varnish with a matt or satin varnish and then 'age' by applying streaks of brown wax polish.

This will age and 'yellow' the surface a little, as well as forming a barrier. Try to leave streaks of bare emulsion as well as bare wood, so that there are three or four differing tones.

When you have painted the design, follow with a coat of water-based varnish, after which the piece might be antiqued (*see page 49*) and then given a coat of oil-based varnish. Alternatively, you might just give it a coat of plain or, for an antiquing effect, tinted wax, or varnish then wax (*see page 49*).

For the same distressed effect, but with a colour rather than the wood showing through a little, paint two coats of an undercolour in emulsion, drying after each, then one coat of the top colour emulsion. Distress the top coat lightly with sandpaper in the same way, to reveal the undercolour.

Wax resist On some surfaces, or when coats of several colours are to be distressed, a 'resist' may be needed to make the distressing easier. For emulsion coats, wax is used where the paint is to be removed; this can be either candle wax or white wax polish, depending on the desired effect.

Nowadays, furniture is often made from medium density fibreboard, a smooth wood-coloured material made from ground twigs. Like chipboard, it has no grain. To create a distressed grainy look, seal it first with shellac. Using one end of a white candle like a crayon, firmly streak over the areas of the surface where the paint is to be removed, going in one direction with the imaginary wood grain; vary the length and width of the streaks to give a random effect rather than a pedestrian crossing! Think of stalactites and stalagmites, each ending in a point rather than squared.

Work from the outer edge of each facet towards the centre. Where possible, work in vertical lines rather than from side to side as the latter tends to result in streaks that curve slightly in a windscreen wiper effect, which detracts from the credibility.

Rub quite hard so that small chips of

WAX RESIST

1 This MDF (medium-density fibreboard) surface has been sealed with shellac and streaked with candle wax in the direction of imaginary grain, this will resist the coat of yellow emulsion, making it easier to distress.

2 When the emulsion has dried, rub lightly with fine or medium sandpaper, working in the direction of the imaginary wood grain, to remove the paint from the waxed areas. Streak over sparingly with shellac to age.

candlewax appear on the surface; cover anything from 40 to 80 per cent of the area, depending on how distressed you want it to look.

Over this, paint your top coat of emulsion. It should cover the surface without being too thick or it will be more difficult to remove, so use the brush with vigour, laying paint on in all directions, then laying it off by lightly and smoothly running the bristles through the wet paint in the direction of the imaginary grain. When the coat is dry, rub lightly all over in the direction of the grain with fine-to-medium sandpaper, gradually increasing the pressure over the waxed areas until you are happy with the effect. The revealed MDF should have the grainy look of wood.

The same method can successfully be used between two contrasting coats of emulsion. Put the first colour on in the same way, brushing with the grain. When dry, streak with a candle; cover with the second colour; dry, and sand.

A word of warning – don't do this in bright sunshine or a hot climate, as the wax can melt under the top coat before sanding, giving a rather different effect!

For a more exaggerated distress, use soft white wax polish instead, putting it on in smears and blobs with a fitch brush, or using a cocktail stick or sponge. Aim again to achieve streaks going with the grain of the wood, real or imaginary, rather than dotted all over, which would not look so convincing. As before, concentrate on places which would logically have been worn over the years.

You can achieve a similar effect between two coats of oil-based paint, using the same technique, but with Vaseline instead of waxes.

Some of the softer paints, such as casein paint and distemper, can be distressed from the top rather than between coats. Apply two coats of emulsion for the undercolour, followed when dry by one coat of the softer paint in a different colour. When dry, rub lightly but fast with fine wire wool, going with the grain; this will 'burnish' the surface giving a beautiful shine and deepening the colour. Put a little wax containing a solvent called toluene on the wire wool and rub just where the top coat is to be removed. The wax will gradually dissolve the soft paint, revealing the colour beneath. Buff up with a soft cloth, and the paint will appear to have the patina of years of cherishing.

Meths rubbing If you want your piece to look grainy, without going back to the wood or undercolour, a very pretty old-looking effect can be achieved by using methylated spirits, the solvent for emulsion, instead of sandpaper.

First, apply three coats of emulsion quite thickly, with the brushmarks going either in the direction of the wood grain or whichever direction is most appropriate for the shape of the piece; allow each coat to dry before applying the next. This colour will be the predominant one, altered only a little by the subsequent coat, which is a thin coat or glaze of a contrasting or antiquing colour.

The glaze is made either by diluting an emulsion of a contrasting or deeper colour with 4–5 parts of water, or by mixing acrylic tube paint with water to the equivalent consistency. When sparingly painted over the basecoat it should appear like a streaky veil of colour, a little stronger than you ultimately want it to be.

When this is completely dry, moisten some paper towel generously with methylated spirit, and lightly rub this over the top coat in the direction of the brushmarks. Do not concentrate on any area for too long, as this would start to dissolve the undercolour, mixing it with and diluting the glaze, rather than just removing it from the tops of the brushmarks. Re-moisten the paper towel frequently, going back over darker areas when they have dried from the first wiping, until you are happy with the effect. Leave the glaze in any indentations or crevices of turned legs or mouldings, blending it outwards but removing more from highlights and edges, the centres of panels and anywhere that might have been dusted frequently. Should you remove too much, it can always be lightly re-applied. Use the meths-damp paper as you would a paint brush, rather than scrubbing! It's the solvent on the paper that does the work, not the paper itself.

Any mixture of colours can be used for this effect, so experiment with dark over light or light over dark, remembering that the amount of contrast can be varied from definite to subtle, the top glaze always affecting the predominant undercolour and changing it slightly (*see mixing colours, page 35*).

For a host of lovely neutral shades, start with three coats of white emulsion or acrylic primer/undercoat, either in one direction, as above, or in a flip-flop manner, in all directions. Cover with a thin glaze of Raw, Green or Burnt Umber, or any neutral mixture. When this is rubbed off with meths, the white is antiqued.

Crackle paint Another extremely distressed paint finish is cracked or crazed paint. This is one of the few finishes that is not so easy to achieve successfully over an entire surface, but can be used very effectively on small areas in conjunction with other distressing techniques. Over a basecoat of emulsion, paint a coat of 'crackle glaze'. Various materials can be used for this (*see page 34*). What they have in common is that they are transparent, water-based and, most importantly, water-soluble when dry.

When the glaze is dry, usually within an hour, a contrast coat of emulsion is applied as quickly and simply as possible, without overbrushing or going back over the wet paint (very difficult, rather like eating a doughnut and not licking the lips). The reason for this is that as the emulsion re-wets the

---

METHS RUBBING

1 Three coats of blue emulsion have been applied to this piece, followed when dry by a sparing coat of dark green emulsion, diluted with 4–5 parts of water (alternatively, use acrylic tube paint in place of emulsion).

2 When dry, moisten a paper towel with methylated spirit. Rub this lightly over the surface, removing dark green from the ridges of the previous brushmarks and leaving it in the dips (re-moisten the towel frequently).

CRACKLE PAINT

Here, dark blue emulsion is applied over yellow on which a coat of crackle glaze has dried. Either brush on the second colour, where possible in 'one stroke' to avoid disturbing the glaze, or stipple it on, as seen at the bottom

non-waterproof crackle glaze, the latter immediately begins to attack and crack the top coat, making it very unstable and vulnerable. If you brush over this already-moving surface, even after only a few seconds, the cracks, still invisible, will turn to porridge, and the only remedy is to wipe it off and start the process from the beginning again. An easier way to apply the top coat of emulsion is to stipple it on with the tip of a brush, which obviates the need to agitate the surface. Provided the paint stipples are close enough to leave no gaps, a crazy paving effect should appear within a few minutes, gradually becoming defined as the paint dries.

Either method can be used in small patches over a larger surface, though you must try to remember where the crackle glaze has been put! When crackle glazing over an oil-based surface, seal first with one of the meths-based lacquers, such as shellac, to make the crackle glaze adhere. The finish must be sprayed or brushed with several coats of oil-based varnish to stabilize it, as water-based varnish might also crack.

WASHES

Let us now turn to those finishes which are created by putting something over the base coat and leaving it as it is. Here, the degree of absorbency of the base coat plays an important part. The sheen of silk vinyl emulsion, for instance, or oil-based eggshell or satin finish paint, have little or no absorbency; matt emulsion will absorb a little; softer surfaces, such as distemper, Plaka or gesso (plaster of Paris), are more porous still, while plaster is completely porous throughout.

In olden days, a wooden surface would often be given several coats of gesso to fill the grain, creating a completely smooth surface after a rub with fine sandpaper. You can still do this by mixing gesso powder with rabbit skin size to the correct consistency, but it takes time and the mixture must be applied with care. Each coat should follow the last just before it is completely dry, or cracks can appear.

A less arduous alternative is to use a soft thick paint, such as distemper or Plaka. It is the binder in a paint that dictates its degree of absorbency. Emulsions are bound by PVA or acrylic, both of which are man-made and have a plastic quality; this means that, like a plastic mac, they are waterproof and designed to resist absorbency. Distemper is bound by casein, which is extracted from milk, and the paint remains porous even when dry. By using two or three coats of a porous paint, one is effectively building up an absorbent layer into which a wash of colour can be fed, rather like painting over blotting paper.

With any of these softer paints, it is important that the drying time of each coat should be as slow as possible, to avoid cracking. If the water content is absorbed too quickly, both into the previous coat as well as the atmosphere, cracks will occur, so make sure you work in a cool environment, waiting until the previous coat is almost dry before applying the next.

After two, three and four coats, depending on the thickness of the paint used, allow the paint to dry completely. You can then either give it a light sanding with fine sandpaper, to produce a really smooth surface, or leave it as it is. Over this you can apply either a wash of watercolour or water-based acrylic tube paint diluted with lots of water, or a glaze of oil-tube paint diluted with white spirit. This will sink into the soft layers, creating an irregular veil of soft streaky colour, rather like a colour wash. If using acrylics, make sure they are very watery to begin with as they dry to a waterproof finish; stronger colour can always be added later. Apply the wash in overlapping streaks, going with the grain and adding water as you go, if neccessary, to soften the effect.

COLOUR-WASH OVER GESSO

Three coats of soft, absorbent paint, such as Plaka or distemper, have been applied, each one being allowed to dry naturally. A wash of Venetian Red acrylic tube paint, with water added to it, is streaked on.

If you have opted for a glaze of oil-tube paint mixed with white spirit; daub it on in streaks with a brush, then moisten some paper towel with white spirit and wipe this over the whole surface, moving it in the same direction as the brushmarks; this will dilute the glaze and force it into the absorbent surface. Leave the surface to dry overnight, then rub with fine sandpaper, again in the direction of the original brushmarks. Finally, burnish the surface with fine wire wool. By using an oil glaze of half-and-half Raw Umber and Raw Sienna over white distemper or Plaka, an effect very like old ivory can be achieved.

For a more sparsely spaced colour wash, first streak the base coat, going in the direction of the original brushstrokes, with either acrylic (water-based) varnish or artists' acrylic medium. Each streak will seal the porous surface, making that part resist the subsequent wash, so that the latter only sinks in where the acrylic var-nish or medium has not been applied.

Plaster Taking absorbency a step further, we come to plaster. This can either be genuine plaster, or composition or plastic mouldings, which can be rendered like plaster by giving them one coat of shellac and about three of a soft, porous white paint.

Of course, these can be painted with an opaque paint so that no one would know they were plaster, but a far softer, prettier effect can be given to such mouldings by making use of their porous quality and painting with a thin wash of acrylic tube paint, mixed with water to a weak tea consistency.

You can apply one colour over the entire surface, but if the moulding has a naturalistic carved design, such as flowers or fruit, you might decide to use several appropriately-coloured washes, choosing shades of green for the leaves, for example, and pink, blue or yellow for flowers. Restrict your palette to the minimum of colours – say three or four – and mix other tones from these. Don't use white paint, as that will immediately make any wash opaque; for palest shades, simply add extra water and allow the white plaster base to shine through.

While that wash is still damp, seal it with shellac. The reason for applying this coat over the damp wash is that shellac dries very quickly; if painted over dry plaster, it will not easily be absorbed, and this can cause ugly runs. It is important to bear in mind when mixing your washes that all the colours will 'yellow' a little when the shellac is put over them; blues will turn towards turquoise, greens become yellower, pinks more coral. This makes the whole thing look more antique, which enhances the end result. If you prefer it to look clean and fresh, seal with sanding sealer or patent knotting, which are paler, or you can even use Unibond glue diluted with a little water – this usually takes longer to dry than the half hour or so required for the shellac family.

POLYCHROME WASHES ON PLASTER

1 This composition moulding has been rendered with three coats of absorbent paint to give a plaster effect. Next, watery washes are applied, the palette being restricted to three acrylic colours; these will soak into the surface.

2 A coat of shellac is now applied; this will seal the coloured washes and yellow them a little, to give an antique effect. Apply fairly generously, allowing the shellac to dribble into the indentations of the carving.

3 To make the moulding look even more convincingly old, paint over it with powdered rottenstone mixed with soft white wax, brushing into the indentations and wiping the surplus off the highlights with a cloth.

Simpler still, for an alabaster look on white plaster, is to wet the surface all over with plain water then seal with shellac or sanding sealer or, for a paler tone, a mixture of the two.

Since plaster-type pieces are usually mainly decorative, such as the mirror frame on *page 107* or the plaster column top on *page 99*, there is no need to seal them with varnish, simply use wax with an additive. Brush this all over the item with a fitch, then wipe off the tops or highlights with paper towel or a cloth, leaving the residue in the dips.

For an antique finish, as seen on the mirror frame, use soft white wax mixed with about half its volume of powdered rottenstone, which looks just like dust. If this is darker than you wish, mix the rottenstone first with the lighter-coloured fullers' earth and then with the wax. The exact amounts will vary, depending on the temperature, as wax is much softer in warm weather and may then need propor-

tionally more powder to make it manageable. For the alabaster look, as on the column, use ready-made liming wax instead. Make sure the wax mixture goes into all the dips and indentations when you put it on, but only wipe off the high places.

Although they are the colours of dark (rottenstone) and light (fullers' earth) dust, these powders are not actual colours in the same sense as powdered pigments. Originally, rottenstone was mixed with linseed oil to a paste and used as the finest of abrasives in the final stages of varnishing a piece. When mixed with wax, these powders do not dissolve as would pigments, which are the pure colour ground to a fine powder from which paints are made. Rottenstone and similar powders, on the other hand, provide substance in the crevices, leaving dusty crustations when the wax dries.

Any of the pigments can also be mixed with soft white wax, altering the colour very slightly, to give a final

tinted film after varnishing. This includes the iridescent pearlized powders, which are available in all the shades found in mother-of-pearl. If the green one, for example, is mixed with white wax and applied over a darker blue-green wash, then buffed up with a soft cloth an hour or so later, the effect will resemble the sheen of a dragonfly.

True ultramarine used to be made by grinding lapis lazuli to a fine powder, and was very expensive to produce. Nowadays, French Ultramarine is made through a cheaper process. Raw Umber is extracted and ground from the earth of Umbria in Italy; if the powder is then cooked on a high heat it changes colour to become the deeper, warmer Burnt Umber.

When using powders, always take the precaution of wearing a mask for protection.

Verdigris effect   Liming wax is white wax with Titanium White powder pigment added to it, and has several uses. As already mentioned, it is particularly

---

VERDIGRIS ON PLASTER

1 Paint bare plaster with a watery wash of acrylic tube paint: mix a metallic colour from Yellow Ochre, Phthalo Blue and a little black, slightly bluer than the eventual colour is to be, to allow for the subsequent coat of shellac.

2 While the wash is still damp, apply the shellac to seal it in. This will turn the original colour more yellow and give it an old look. For a paler alternative, use a sanding sealer or even Unibond glue diluted with water.

3 Mix Veridian and Payne's Grey oil tube paint with liming wax to a verdigris colour. Paint over the dry shellac, taking care to brush into the crevices, and wiping off the raised areas with paper towel to create highlights.

good over the water and shellac finish, or with a plain pale wash rather than several colours. Again, it is applied all over with a fitch, especially into dips and crevices, then wiped off as before, just on the highlights.

All waxes can be mixed with oil-tube paint instead of powder, to tint them. Liming wax mixed with any colour will produce a pastel colour because of the wax's white content. To obtain the colour of verdigris, for instance, mix about 6mm (¼in) of Veridian Green and 3mm (⅛in) of Payne's Grey into about a tablespoon of liming wax. Used over a bronze-coloured or blue/black wash, this can look very like the real thing. Similarly, liming wax, when mixed with white pearlized powder and used over a black base, can give the lustred look of old pewter when polished.

STAINS

Where we would use a wash for plaster, a wash-type colour used for wood would be termed a stain. As before, it is the absorbency of the wood which is important, so the stain can sink into the surface, rather than sitting on top. For this reason only new or stripped old wood can be treated in this way. If you have to strip a piece, you will find that an electric sander can be a great help on flat surfaces; alternatively, solvents can be used (*see page 15*).

If your piece is darker than you wish once you have stripped back to the bare wood, it can be made paler by bleaching, with or without staining afterwards. Good decorators' merchants stock various specialist wood bleaches for which the manufacturer's instructions should be followed.

Most new wooden furniture is made from pine, which is pale in colour and so does not need to be bleached. On the other hand, it can look wonderful if stained a pastel colour.

Emulsion The word 'stain' conjures up dark wood colours in various shades of brown. Certainly these can be used, as for the sideboard on *page*

72, but a pretty alternative is to use emulsion paint, diluted with from four to six parts of water, depending on the thickness of the paint. Paint this on sparingly and allow it to sink into the wood; if it looks too opaque, wipe some off when it is half dry, using paper towel and going along the grain. Any colour can be used, but the prettiest effects are achieved when the colour contrasts with the wood so that the hard grain, which absorbs less than the soft grain, still looks wood coloured; for example, blues, greens and greys look wonderful over the pale gold of pine.

If you want a two-tone effect, as on this page, mix the two colours separately with water to the right consistency and work on one facet at a time; paint the lighter one all over, allowing it to half dry. Wipe off streaks along the grain to reveal the wood, using paper towel. If the stain 'puddles' at the end of a streak, let it dry a little more, or mop off the surplus and re-streak.

Next, apply the second colour by streaking it over the first colour in places, over the revealed wood in others, or where the two join. Try to make the streaks random, varying the length and width, lifting the brush at the end of each to leave a point, and always going in the direction of the grain. Allow the second colour to half dry, then lightly blend the edges of these streaks with paper towel wrapped firmly round your forefinger, remembering to tuck the rest of the towel into the palm of your hand so it does not disturb your work.

When the stain is dry, it must be sealed with sanding sealer or acrylic varnish so that any subsequent treatment does not sink in. Water tends to open up the grain of wood, so you may need to lightly sand when the sealer is dry, using fairly fine sandpaper. At this stage a design or stencil can be applied and then sealed again. The next option is either to varnish with oil- or water-based varnish, or to 'lime' the piece.

Liming Liming is designed to sit in the grain of the wood rather than on the whole surface, giving a pastel effect. Some woods, such as oak, have excellent grain while others, such as pine, do not. In order to open up the grain, or create grain where there is little or none, use a wire brush. Drag the

1 Bare oak, before and after treatment with a two-part bleach, specially formulated for wood. This takes several hours or overnight.

3 Using emulsion and water, add streaks of a contrasting 'stain', giving them pointed ends; when half dry, blend the edges with paper towel.

length of it firmly along in the direction of the grain once or twice, going over the whole surface; it makes a horrid noise, but will help to open up existing grain or create an imitation.

To lime, either liming wax or liming paste can be used. The choice is largely governed by whether the piece will need to be varnished or not, as varnish can only be applied over the paste. For kitchens, bathrooms and floors the latter is therefore preferable, whereas for bedroom furniture or decorative items, the wax is adequate.

Liming wax comes ready mixed in a tin or you can mix your own by adding Titanium White powder pigment to soft white wax. Test the mixture as you add the powder - the proportions depend on the temperature in which you are working and the desired strength of colour.

Using a cloth or paper towel and taking one facet at a time, rub the wax in a

BLEACHING, STAINING AND LIMING

2 Paint on a stain of emulsion mixed with 4-5 parts water; wait until it is half dry, then use a paper towel to streak the emulsion off in places.

4 Seal with sanding sealer; when dry, lightly draw a wire brush along the grain to open it then, rubbing in a circular motion, apply liming wax.

5 Using paper towel and driving the wax into the grain, liming wax is applied in a circular motion all over the surface. Remove the surplus by wiping

firmly along the grain with a clean cloth. To remove more wax, moisten the cloth with white spirit, taking care not to remove wax from the grain.

circular motion all over the surface, so that it is driven into all the little pores, grain, and any blemishes. As soon as the surface is covered, wipe off the surplus with clean paper towel, going in the direction of the grain and leaving the white liming wax only in the indented lines of the wood. If it dries so quickly that you cannot remove as much as you would like, moisten some clean paper towel with white spirit or turpentine, and gently wipe with the grain to dissolve a little more wax, then use a dry piece of paper towel to remove the dissolved wax, being careful not to take it from the grain.

After a few hours, when the wax has dried, it can be polished with a cloth to give a soft sheen. It is not usually necessary to seal over the wax, as it will gradually harden over about two weeks. If you wish to protect it, you cannot use varnish, but you can apply two coats of white polish (see page 14) after that time, drying between the coats. If the polish is too shiny, you can rub gently with fine wire wool to make it more matt, and perhaps re-wax with ordinary wax polish.

The liming wax can be tinted with oil-tube paint, but because of its white content this will produce pastel colours – imagine pale blue or grey grain in natural oak which has been sealed as described above with sanding sealer.

Liming paste is like a thick white emulsion but is water soluble when dry; it also can be tinted with pigments, acrylic tube paint or gouache, like the chair and cages on page 96. Seal the surface as above, if necessary, then paint the white or tinted paste all over it; do not lay it on too thickly. When dry, take a water-damp cloth and simply wipe off the surplus, leaving it just in the grain of wood or in the indentations of items such as carvings or mouldings. Use an oil- rather than water-based varnish to seal it, remembering that it is not waterproof. One or two coats are generally enough, though you may need more for floors.

GLAZES

Many wonderful effects can be created by using slow-drying scumble glaze over a mid-sheen base coat. The glaze, which is virtually colourless, is tinted with tube colour or stainers to give a transparent film of that colour; this allows the undercolour to show through and, because it is slow drying, it can be moved around to create a finish, all sorts of different tools being used to create different effects.

Originally, scumble glaze was always oil-based, but in recent years, acrylic scumbles have been developed by the addition of retarders. The acrylic (water-based) scumble glazes are much more pleasant to use and do not yellow with time, but they dry a little more quickly than their oil-based counterparts. The water-based scumble has been used for all our glaze finishes, including marbleizing and tortoiseshell.

Where to start? There are so many possibilities! As for all glaze finishes, the base coat should be mid-sheen – either an oil-based satin finish paint or water-based silk vinyl (see pages 12–13). The colour you choose will still dominate after the glaze has been put on, so think about the depth of colour you want and experiment with differing base coats. For example, any coloured glaze will give a considerable contrast over white; and the finish will appear quite definite. If, on the other hand, the base coat is a lighter tone of the glaze, the finish will look more subtle (see the kitchen top on page 83). Alternatively, a contrasting undercolour can make the same glaze look completely different. Red over yellow ocre will glow with light and an orangey warmth; red over pale green will be dulled by the green, its complementary colour (see pages 35–7).

To mix your desired colour of acrylic scumble, squeeze about 12mm (½ in) of gouache, acrylic tube-paint or a small amount of stainer into a container and dilute with a teaspoonful or so of water to make it runnier and more easily mixed with the glaze.

Gouache and stainers give stronger colouring than acrylic tubes. Add a tablespoon of glaze and, having mixed it up, test the colour on a small section of the project – if it is too strong in colour, add some more glaze and try again; if too pale, add more paint, again having diluted it with the water. Each test should be wiped off the surface as soon as possible.

Once you are happy with the colour, you can multiply the quantities up and mix enough for the entire project. The rate of coverage is usually mentioned on the manufacturer's label.

Bagging Perhaps the easiest finish of all is 'Bagging'! When your mid-sheen basecoat is dry, lay on a tinted glaze, brushing it out in all directions so it is reasonably even; cover the whole of a small facet, such as a drawer, at a time.

With larger areas, cover a patch about 30–60cm (12–24in) each way at one time, leaving a ragged rather than straight edge, ready to overlap the next patch. Turn a plastic supermarket bag inside out; scrumple it up into a ball, and pat the crumpled side into the wet glaze, each pat just overlapping the last. Turn your hand in the air a little between pats, to avoid repeating the pattern. The sooner you do this after applying the glaze, the more definite the impression of the crumples will be. To reduce the impression, go over the surface a second time with the bag.

Dragging With dragging, which is another lovely glaze finish, it is best to put the glaze on sparingly in dragged parallel brushmarks, usually going with the grain of the wood, and immediately drag over them again with a dry brush. To drag, press the length of the bristles into the glaze, with the brush at a low angle to the surface; move your whole body in the direction of the drag, enabling the handle to stay at this angle.

Ragging Ragging is particularly pretty under stencilling. Because much of the glaze is removed, it is softer and subtler than bagging or dragging. Use stockinette, sold by decorators' merchants or car shops. Cut an appropriate length from the roll; shake thoroughly to get rid of loose bits of knitting that might stick to the glaze, then turn it inside out. Apply the glaze in the same way as for bagging, a section at a time. Fold the stockinette into a pad and pat into the wet glaze, scuffing and smudging it a little in a different direction with each pat, to give a blurred look. Because the stockinette is very absorbent, much of the glaze will be removed, leaving just a veil of colour, coming and going.

Frottage On the face of it, this sounds like a ridiculous finish! Meaning 'rubbing' in French, the technique creates the impression of a rough surface, such as old plaster, on a smooth surface, the exact effect depending on the colours used. For this we need plenty of old newspapers, or perhaps unprinted newspaper, which has no creases in it. Again lay the glaze on in all directions, glazing a patch slightly larger than the newspaper to be used. Immediately cover it with a flat piece of newspaper, leaving the edges of the glaze showing; try to avoid air bubbles under it – not always easy! Smooth all over the paper with your hands (not too hard or the print may appear in the glaze); lift one side of the paper, and peel it off. It should leave a mouldy-looking surface beneath, full of texture and dribble marks! Paint the next patch of glaze to overlap the last up to the edge where the newspaper lay and repeat the process. Diagonal patches, as on the kichen top on *page 83*, may be better than horizontal ones. The absorbency or lack of it in the 'tool' you use will always affect the density of the end result. For instance in bagging, the plastic bag is completely non-absorbent so the glaze is simply rearranged rather than any being removed, whereas with ragging and frottage, the cloth or paper removes most of the glaze, giving a much paler end result.

Another way of reducing the density is to add a little water to the tinted glaze, making it thinner and therefore easier to remove. This can be an advantage when ragging or frottaging, but may speed up the drying time a little; where more definition is needed, such as for dragging, it is better to leave the glaze undiluted.

RAGGING	FROTTAGE
	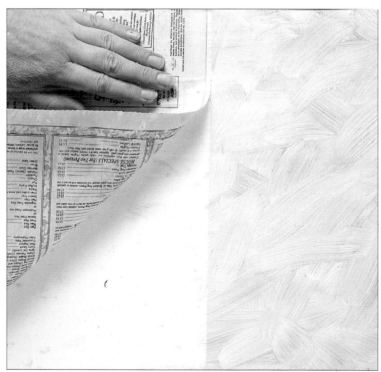

Apply tinted glaze over a mid-sheen base coat. Using stockinette, pat the surface all over, taking off some of the glaze, and simultaneously smudging the remainder by pushing it in different directions.

Add a little water to the glaze and brush it over the surface. Place a sheet of newspaper over the wet glaze, smoothing it flat with your hands; peel it off, leaving a mottled texture on the surface.

Marbleizing Because acrylic glaze is slow drying, it is ideal for 'marbleizing'. I use the term marbleizing rather than marbling because with marbling there is an exact recipe for each marble, each as different as 'Coq au vin' and 'Crepe suzette' in the cookery world. Marbleizing, however, can be worked in any colour or colours and is much less complicated. This method was used on the wine table on *page 52*.

Start with a palette with small squeezes of the gouache or acrylic colours that you want to use arranged round the edge of a disposable paper or white china plate. Untinted glaze is put into a container such as a jam jar and mixed with the paint on the plate as you go.

To achieve the misty, blended look of marble, the whole surface must be made wet, either by covering with plain glaze first and then feeding it with colour, or, as here, covering the

MARBLEIZING

1 Several different colours and shades of glaze, from palest to darkest in order, are painted in irregular diagonal drifts over the basecoat.

2 Pat over the wet surface with stockinette, from dark to light, to remove surplus glaze and colour, leaving a mottled surface.

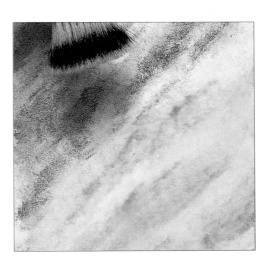

3 Sweep lightly back and forth over the surface in all directions, using an upright badger brush to blur and blend the transparent colours.

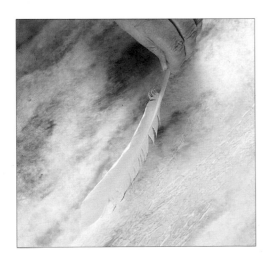

4 Draw the side of a feather through the glaze in places, tapping and tugging, and changing the angle slightly in a trellis effect. Soften with the badger.

5 Dip a fine brush in meths; draw the tip through the glaze in both straight and erratic bursts, roughly following the diagonal, making light veins.

6 Soften in one direction at right angles across the veins, then stroke the length of them lightly, sinking them into their surroundings.

surface with differing shades and colours of glaze so that no part is left dry. Using a 12mm (½in) decorator's brush, take a blob of glaze and mash it on your palette. With the tips of the bristles, draw a very little of the lightest-coloured paint into the blob of glaze and mix. The glaze must be transparent, so do not add too much paint; it is easier to add later than to take away. Daub this in random drifts diagonally across the area, holding the brush on its side, almost horizontal to the surface, at right angles to the direction in which you are going.

Rather than painting, roll the brush away from or towards you, altering the pressure to achieve drifts varying from thin to thick, or visa versa. Leave room between drifts for other colours or tones to be added. Take a little more neat glaze, add it to the original puddle, and draw in more of the same colour to make a deeper tone; add this in places, still rolling the brush on.

Change, perhaps, to a different colour by putting some more glaze on the palette in a new place and adding the new colour to it as before. Roll this into some of the blank spaces, the drifts always following the same diagonal; deepen some areas as before, then mix some of the new colour with the first to create yet another colour, until all is covered, and there are no gaps.

Using stockinette as for ragging (*see page 27*), gently blot the surface all over, working from light to dark, reducing the thickness and strength of colour. Next, use a badger or hog softener brush to blend and blur the glazes. Hold it straight upright, swinging from the elbow with an immobile wrist so that only the flat tips of the bristles very lightly touch the surface – someone once described it charmingly as 'kissing the surface'! – this may need a bit of practice. The upright brush sweeps should go back and forth across almost the entire surface. After two or three sweeps, allow your wrist to re-direct the brush to a new angle, about 45 or 50 degrees to the first, cre-

ating an effect resembling plaiting or herringbone. Don't overdo the blurring at this stage, as each subsequent softening affects the first layer of glaze.

Take a goose feather and run your fingers from top to bottom, ruffling one side. Following the same diagonal as the original drifts, tap the ruffled side lengthways into the darkest areas of glaze, tugging it a little towards you during each tap. Repeat this across the piece on the diagonal in a narrow drift and/or in V-shapes, varying the angle slightly, like a rose trellis, to create the very fine web of veins found in many marbles. Soften these with the badger or hog brush, herringboning down their length.

Next, dip a small long-haired brush into meths. Carefully and lightly draw the tip through the glaze on the same diagonal, to create negative veins. These can either run in straight lines, angling to change direction, or they can branch; they never curve in a wavy line. Fidget the brush in places to give ragged, erratic sections. Don't be tempted to cover the surface with veins – it is more realistic to have random skeins going from one edge to the other on the diagonal or tailing off. These can again be softened with the badger, either in all directions or just across, all in the same direction; this last causes the glaze to build up on one side, and is finished with a light stroke the length of the vein.

If you go wrong, or a bristle falls on the surface, don't panic! Wipe the brush; gently remove the hair with a corner of it, then pat the blemish with the cloth and soften over it. When dry, seal with several coats of water-based satin varnish, then at least two of oil-based varnish, lightly sanding with fine sandpaper before the final coat.

Tortoiseshell Now we come to one of my special favourites. It is a constant source of amazement to me that blobs of paint and glaze can turn themselves into something as indefinable as tortoiseshell, with a little help from the badger brush!

The base for tortoiseshell is either a yellow mid-sheen paint or gold; Dutch metal leaf can be used. The palette of colours, to be mixed with glaze in the same way as for marbleizing, is Raw Sienna, Burnt Sienna, Burnt Umber and a little black. Gouache gives stronger colouring than acrylic tube-paint, though the latter can be used for paler versions of tortoiseshell.

Paint the whole yellow or gold surface with uncoloured glaze using a 12mm (½in) decorators' or varnish brush. On your palette, mix a little Raw Sienna into a blob of glaze, using the same brush and making sure the glaze colour is very pale and transparent. Decide on the shell's diagonal and, holding the brush at right angles to that diagonal, roll on elongated discs of coloured glaze, about the size of quails' eggs, leaving some space between each. Next, add Burnt Sienna, which is a very strong reddish pigment, and Burnt Umber to a new blob of glaze, and put this on in smaller egg-shapes, some between and some overlapping the first shapes.

Change to a smaller brush, such as a fitch and, with fresh glaze, mix just Burnt Umber with perhaps a touch of black. Still thinking of the original diagonal, daub irregular streaks over and between the existing glazes, making angular 'S' shapes, 'Y's and 'T's – almost like hieroglyphics. About two-thirds to three-quarters of the surface should now be covered, but there should still be pale yellow patches shining through.

The manner of softening tortoiseshell is all-important. Holding the softener as for marbleizing, first sweep gently all over in the direction of the original diagonal. Next, sweep backwards, in the opposite direction. Thirdly, sweep in one direction, at right angles to these, then fourthly, in the opposite direction to the third, finally going back to the first direction – south, north, east, west and south again. Next, mix some black, with a little less glaze this time. Small flurries of dabs and blobs here and there will accentuate the colour; still work on the diagonal and avoid spacing them too evenly. Soften again lightly in all the original directions. Look at your work and decide whether it needs to be darker or lighter. If it needs to be darker, add some Burnt Umber and glaze; if lighter, wipe the brush and use uncoloured glaze to open up areas, softening again afterwards. When dry, varnish as for marbleizing.

Speed is fairly important for both marbleizing and tortoiseshell, so if you are not satisfied, wipe off and try again. Practice makes perfect and each time you will get quicker – so the results should get better and better!

TORTOISESHELL

1 After diagonal egg-shaped daubs of Raw Sienna glaze, paint smaller ovals of a Burnt Sienna and Umber glaze mixture both between and over-lapping them.

2 Mixing them with a little black, and haphazardly overlapping existing colours, add smaller, angular Y-, L- and S-shaped marks in Burnt Umber glaze, still thinking of the diagonal.

3 Using a badger brush, soften the marks in the direction of the diagonal (south), then work north and east, followed by west and finally the south diagonal again.

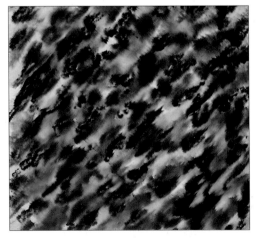

4 Mix some glaze with black, adding slightly more paint; using a smaller brush than the first, such as a fitch, dab the deeper colour in places, unevenly, to darken the effect.

5 Soften with the badger brush, again working in all directions. If the effect is too light, add more Burnt Umber glaze in places; if too dark, use an untinted glaze, and soften again.

FINISHING TOUCHES
In both marbleizing and tortoiseshell we have used the brushes to simulate nature so that the beholder is deceived into believing they could be looking at the real thing! When any finish is dry, you may wish to alter or darken the colour; for instance, should your tortoiseshell be too pale it can be darkened by varnishing with a tinted varnish, such as one of the ready-mixed wood colours (dark oak, for example). Alternatively, tint ordinary oil-based varnish with oil-tube paint; mash about 12mm (½in) of the oil paint with a little white spirit, then add the varnish and stir gently to avoid causing bubbles. Test a small section before applying to the whole surface.

SPECIAL EFFECTS

All sorts of wonderful effects can be achieved with the addition of two further possibilities to those already described. The first is texture: if, instead of a smooth painted surface, we create one that is rough, we can imitate anything from old plaster to stone slabs. Texture can be given to a surface in many different ways, each with its own effect, and as a further option colour can be mixed into the texture or painted over it.

SIMPLE TEXTURE

The simplest way to create a texture is to add some powdered filler or whiting to emulsion. When painted on, this will give a grainy look to a surface, and the more you add, the rougher the surface will become. The textured paint can either be put on all in one direction, with the grain of the wood, or in a flip-flop manner rather like basket weave, giving a more random effect. These textures will be more evident if coated with a thin wash of either emul-sion or oil-tube paint which, when dry, is then partially removed by the appropriate solvent or sandpaper, respectively, leaving the undercolour exposed on the highlights.

For a more extreme texture, ready-mixed filler (spackle), with no paint added, can be applied with a brush. It is quite stiff, so you will need to use an old brush and quite a lot of strength! Before it begins to dry, brush over the surface again to ensure that the peaks and dips remain.

The second possibility is gilding. Most of us reach for gold wax or dip into gold paint without dreaming how easy and much more exciting it is to use real leaf. There are two meth-ods of applying leaf: water gilding, which takes years of experience, and oil or mordent gilding, which is compara-tively easy. With a little practice, we can all enjoy the plea-sure of using real gold or its cheaper but equally effective counterpart, Dutch metal leaf.

To give a stone-like effect (*as seen on the conservatory table on page 97*), start by applying ready-mixed fine-surface filler in random patches. Stipple these with a wire brush while wet to create peaks. A layer of the mixture is then spread around the peaks with a brush, which is moved in sweeping curves like a fast running river, overlapping the initial patches a little.

When the filler has dried, rub off the sharpest peaks with medium sand-paper, to avoid chipping later, and

---

CREATING TEXTURE

1 Rub the surface (here, Melamine) with wet-and-dry paper to key it, then seal with shellac. Mix powdered Polyfilla into white emulsion and paint it on, brushing in one direction.

2 When this has dried, make a glaze from about 2.5cm (1in) of oil-tube paint (here, Raw Umber), mixed to the consistency of tea with 2–3 tablespoons of white spirit, and paint this all over.

3 Let the glaze dry overnight, then rub lightly with fine-to-medium sandpaper, which will make the surface more smooth, removing glaze from the peaks and leaving it in the dips.

sparingly paint over a coat of emulsion, in the colour of your choice. This coat must not go into all the indentations; it should lie mainly on the tops of the texture, leaving the crevices white.

When dry, paint over a glaze of oil-tube paint mixed with white spirit to the consistency of coffee. Allow this to be absorbed into all the nooks and crannies, wiping it off the peaks with paper towel as you go, before it dries.

By using a glaze of Raw Umber oil-tube paint over a pale blue emulsion, an effect very like turquoise stone can be achieved, and where the glaze dribbles into the white dips, it almost gives an impression of gold.

Textured verdigris Gilding can be used in conjuction with texture. Leaf, applied over a rough surface, can add to the aged look when it has been antiqued, and a texture applied over a flat gilded surface can look wonderful, either when put on and then partly removed, to reveal the gold beneath, or when the texture is one, such as crackle paint (*see pages 20–21*), that allows some of the gold to show through. Seal the gilded surface with one of the meths-based lacquers, such as shellac, before applying the crackle glaze, in order to make it adhere.

The Dutch metal leaf used for the gold undersurface comes in books of twenty-five sheets, 14cm (5½in) square. These are either loose or transfer, the latter being easier to handle, since each sheet is attached to a piece of greased paper. Imitation silver (called Aluminium leaf) and copper are also obtainable in books of the same size. Real gold and silver come in books 9.5cm (3¾in) square; the silver is much the same price as the aluminium, but the real gold is considerably more expensive than the imitation.

For verdigris over Dutch metal leaf, mix Burnt Umber powder pigment into the filler until it is a medium brown colour (it dries a little darker); stipple this over the gilded surface, using a brush with bristles trimmed to about half the full length. Take a good

TEXTURED VERDIGRIS

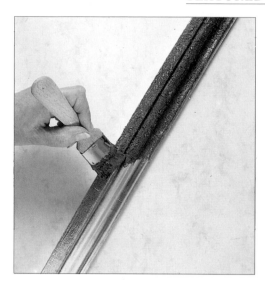

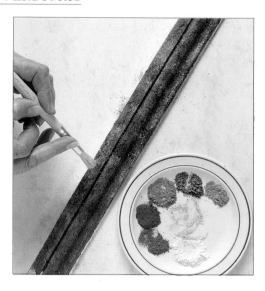

1 *Trim the bristles of a brush to half their original length, then take a scoop of ready-mixed fine surface filler, mixed to a mid-brown with Burnt Umber powder pigment, and stipple it firmly over a gilded moulding.*

2 *Sprinkle the still wet, uneven surface with an assortment of blue, green and white powder colours, tapping them on from above with a fitch and overlapping the drifts of colour only slightly, so they retain their identity.*

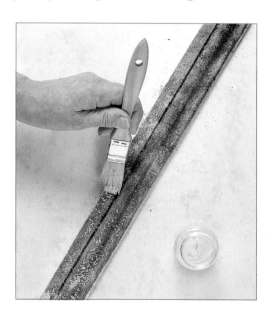

3 *After about ten minutes drying time, very lightly paint on a pale greeny-grey emulsion, giving a bloom that touches the peaks of the texture without actually disturbing the powders too much.*

4 *When the top layer is dry, but the brown filler is only half dry, wrap a paper towel firmly around your forefinger and wipe off a ragged line, varying the pressure as you wipe, to reveal the gold beneath.*

brushful at a time and, holding the brush upright, stab the mixture firmly all over the surface until it adheres. Leave as many peaks as possible, then use a fitch to sprinkle drifts of powdered pigment over it. Select a range of pale greens and blues, such as Cerulean, Terre Vert, Lime Green and Cobalt, mixing some with Titanium White, and adding white on its own.

Dip the brush in the powder and then tap it above the sticky surface, spreading drifts of powder in the various colours until the surface is almost completely covered in a patchwork of blues and greens. After about ten minutes, sparingly paint on a pale greeny-grey emulsion, just lightly skimming the peaks. Don't worry if this blends with the powder colour.

Allow to dry a little more – between ten and twenty minutes – until the filler is fairly dry on top but still moist beneath, then wrap some paper towel round your forefinger and firmly wipe off the mixture just on the raised sections of the moulding, varying the pressure to give a ragged line that reveals the gold. (A word of warning: if the surface is still too wet, it will smear and give too neat a line; if too dry, it will be difficult to remove the filler and you may take off the underlying gold as well.) When dry, the finished surface should be given two or three mists with a spray varnish to seal in any remaining loose powder.

GILDING

To produce a smooth gilded surface rather than a textured one, the traditional method is to start with several coats of gesso. When dry, this is rubbed completely smooth with fine grade sandpaper, and then coated with a red/brown, black or yellow ochre paint, called 'bole'. Ready-made acrylic gesso is available, but is harder to sand than gesso made in the traditional manner by mixing gesso powder with rabbit skin size.

An alternative to these is to use three or four coats of a thick, soft

ANTIQUED GILDING

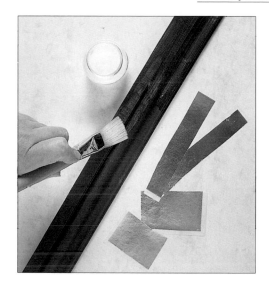

1 Paint a prepared surface with red/brown emulsion; when dry, sparingly brush on a water-based gold-size. The milky-looking goldsize will turn transparent after about fifteen minutes, when it is ready for the leaf.

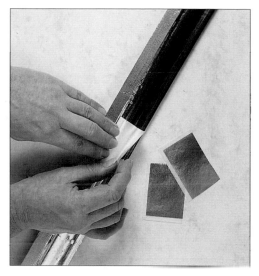

2 Cut the leaf to size and cover the back of the moulding from the outside, tucking the inner edge into the crevice. Next, lay a piece in the crevice and, supporting it, curve it downwards to avoid cracking.

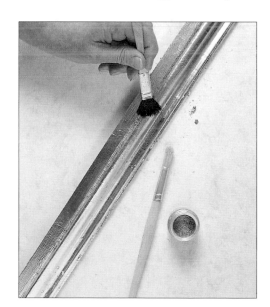

3 When all is covered, smooth over with cotton wool or a soft brush. Pat matching gold-bronze power into any gaps with a fitch. Dry overnight, then brush away the loose overlaps with a soft brush or cotton wool.

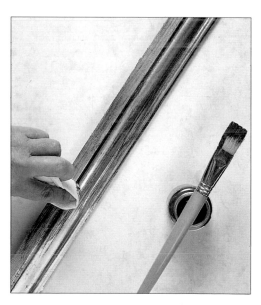

4 To antique it lightly, paint brown emulsion over areas of 5–7.5cm (2–3in) at a time, either wiping some off immediately with paper towel, or patting it off with crumpled paper towel for a sponged look.

paint, such as distemper, which can be sanded and 'burnished' with fine wire wool when dry. The paint can either be the 'bole' colour of your choice, or white. If the latter, then it is followed, after sanding, by a coat of emulsion in the appropriate colour. If the leaf is to be distressed or covered with a texture, you will only require one or two coats of emulsion, lightly sanded.

Once the surface is ready, a sparing coat of goldsize is applied to it. This enables the leaf to adhere to the surface. You can either use an oil-based 3-hour goldsize or a water-based one, which is ready to be leafed after only fifteen minutes.

The leaf must be laid in overlapping sections. Use whole sheets for a large area, and cut the leaf in smaller pieces for smaller areas, cutting each piece a little larger than the area, and leaving it attached to its backing.

Place a section of leaf, gold side down, on the tacky surface; firmly smooth it flat with your fingers, and remove the paper backing. Repeat the process with the next piece, overlapping the first by about 6mm (¼in). When the entire surface has been covered, smooth it over with cotton wool or a squirrel brush, working from the last piece back to the first, to avoid disturbing the overlaps. They may stretch a little, and look untidy, but they must be left in place overnight, while the size dries.

To prevent the leaf cracking in the dips of mouldings such as the one shown here, the flat part was gilded first, the leaf being cut a little deeper than the area to be covered. It was laid on from the outside edge first, the inner edge being tucked into the crevice. Next, the concave area was laid, starting in the crevice, with the leaf supported in the hand so that it could be curved down into the dip and out at the further edge.

If a piece of leaf does crack, lay another piece on top, and press down firmly; if the cracks are too small for this, or there are other small gaps that need filling, use a fitch to cover these with matching gold powder. Leave all the overlaps and powder in place overnight to dry, then rub them to remove all the loose bits, using either cotton wool or the side of a squirrel brush, and rubbing in a circular motion.

CRACKLE VARNISHING

This is a wonderful antiquing finish. Two coats of glue are used, reacting with each other to cause the cracks. First apply 3-hour goldsize sparingly all over (it will go over oil-, water- or spirit-based media). It is quite thick, so make the brush work hard; dip it into the pot only about a quarter to a third of the way up the bristles, spreading out each application as far as possible.

This coat must then dry for two to six hours, until it is dry to the touch but still tacky when pressed firmly with your finger. If in doubt, wait. If it feels completely dry even when pressed, you should still achieve cracks, but they may be finer or smaller.

When you are happy that the surface is ready, apply a fairly sparing coat of water-based liquid gum arabic (if the coat is very thick, the cracks will be extra deep and there is a danger of wrinkles as well as cracks). Once you have painted it on, lightly massage the wet surface with the flats of your fingers for a few minutes. This will help the second coat to cling to the first. Reflect a light over the surface to check that it is absolutely smooth and flawless before you stop massaging.

It usually takes about half an hour for this coat to dry completely, but up to two weeks for all the cracks to appear on the dry surface. To speed it up, leave it overnight or longer in a warm dry atmosphere (damp and humidity can be detrimental) then apply gentle heat by waving a hair dryer a few inches from the surface. The cracks appear slowly, like cracking ice; they are almost invisible, but if you shine a light along the surface, you will detect an unevenness which indicates success. Beware of overheating as this can cause the surface to peel. To make the cracks show, rub over the surface with either oil-tube paint or a powder, such as dust-coloured rotten-stone or gold or silver metallic powders.

Squeeze a little oil-tube paint – usually Raw or Burnt Umber, but experiment with other colours – on one facet. Using kitchen paper moistened with white spirit to dilute the oil slightly, massage all over the surface in a circular motion to drive it into the cracks and crevices. Wipe off the surplus with dry paper towel, leaving as much as you feel appropriate. The more you take off, the more the cracks will be defined. If using a powder, brush it on sparingly with the tip of a fitch or a piece of velvet wrapped round a finger.

Everyone's interpretation of the word 'sparingly' is different, so before crackling a piece of furniture on which you may have spent much time, experiment on a sample board. A wood off-cut or piece of card will do; as you paint the furniture, copy each process on the sample board. Paint two or three separate strips of the 3-hour goldsize on to it, maybe diluting one with a little white spirit, thus enabling a thinner coat to be applied. Write down the time against each, then apply the second coat at 3-hourly intervals in strips running across the first ones. When warmed and antiqued, you should have several options to choose from!

Allow the piece to dry at least overnight, then seal the cracks in with oil-based varnish, since the top coat is water soluble even when dry. It can sometimes produce more cracks even after sealing, so it is best to apply two to three coats.

None of the varnishes are completely heat proof, but most are heat resistant. Use gloss, such as yacht varnish, for maximum protection, lightly sanding when dry, then (for a less shiny effect) use satin or matt oil-based varnish on top.

CHOOSING COLOURS

Colour, and the sheer enormity of its wondrous spectrum, are among the most exciting gifts we have - who hasn't stopped still, lost in the beauty of an amazing sunset, or derived a pang of sheer joy at the sight of a rainbow against a darkened sky, or marvelled at the tones of an impressionist painting?

Choosing colours and working out how to mix them are enormous subjects all on their own! People often ask how to mix colours, as if there were some magic recipe that could be learnt in a morning. I wish this was so, but using colour is rather like learning to cook, even after you have gathered years of experience there is still more to learn, and new recipes to try out. Mixing colours is inevitably time consuming, and it can very often take almost as long to mix an exact colour as to do the actual job.

Learning how to put colours together is also like learning to play a musical instrument, for colours, too, can blend in harmonious chords, just like musical notes.

The knowledge of how colours affect each other comes from experience, and because this is such a help when choosing colours, the best way to approach colour is by experimenting. Mix basic colours; get to know the names of each colour; make your own 'colour wheel' or chart, and generally play with colour. Don't be frightened! it's not as difficult as it sounds and there are a few guidelines that will help.

GENERAL GUIDELINES

All colours can be reproduced from quite a small 'palette'. The choice of the most appropriate medium for a particular project (see pages 12–14) can also affect the look of the finished colour, as certain finishes reflect the light, while others absorb it.

The choice of colour for a project is largely a matter of individual taste. We all like different things, thank goodness, but questions worth asking yourself include the following: where is it to go; how large is it; what proportion of the room will it occupy; do you want the finished item distressed and old-looking or new and pristine?

All these decisions are enough to put us off starting, but they are not as horrendous as they sound. Taking the first into consideration - where is the finished piece to go? Obviously, if it is to fit into an existing colour scheme, your choice will be largely governed by that scheme, and you will choose a colour to match or harmonize with something already in the room. You might, for example, select a lighter or darker tone of a colour in the curtains, which was how the colour for the bedside tables on *page 107* was chosen. If the project is a large one, and you don't want it to overpower the room, aim for a pale colour, such as the neutral finish used for the bedroom cupboard on *page 100*, keeping stronger colours for smaller items, such as lamps or wastepaper bins.

If the paint is to be distressed, bear in mind the colour of the wood or undercolour, and the contrast between that and the distressed top coat. White gives too severe a contrast when distressed over dark wood, so in this case it would be better to aim for a middle to darker tone; equally, a dark colour distressed over pale pine looks less than convincing unless the whole thing is thoroughly antiqued.

Another useful tip when considering a distressed paint finish is to imagine yourself going back in time - decide in which era the object might have been painted, and research which colours were fashionable at the time, being guided by colour charts from companies that make old or historic paint colours (*see page 126*).

MIXING COLOURS

For a large project, it is worth investing in a tin, big enough to do the job, of ready-mixed paint chosen from a colour chart, but for smaller projects you may only need a few spoonfuls of paint. In this case, the best thing is to buy four or five small tins of emulsion: a strong deep blue, yellow and two shades of red, one veering towards orange, like the Cadmium Red in the wheel, and the other towards crimson. (If you are feeling really extravagant, you could invest in two yellows and two blues, as near to those in the colour wheel as possible). Add to these a small tin of brown - the best would be Raw Umber or a colour close to it - and a larger tin of white acrylic primer/undercoat. This last can be used as a primer or undercoat and also mixed with the other colours for paler shades.

A COLOUR WHEEL

Now you have the ingredients for literally hundreds of colours! By looking at the colour-wheel (*see page 36*) I hope you will see this for yourself. For this particular wheel, I have taken two shades each of the three primary colours - blue, yellow and red.

In pure colour theory, there are only the three primaries; the reason why I have taken six primaries for the wheel is because with only one of each, it would not have been possible to create all the colours I wanted. Purple, for example, requires French Ultramarine as opposed to Phthalo blue, though the

In the centre are primary, secondary and tertiary colours; next, each colour has been mixed with a little of its opposite or complementary colour; adding white to these produces the subtle tones of the outer wheel.

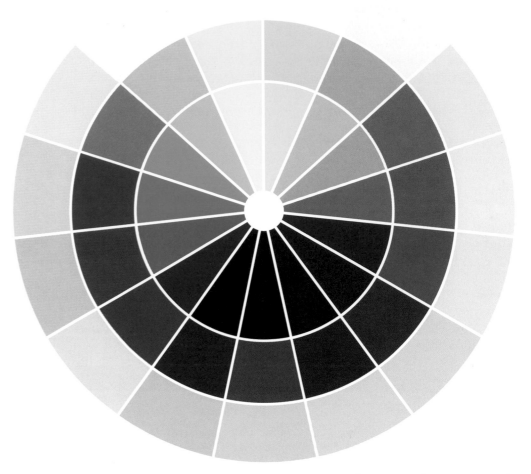

latter is better for mixing to make greens; similarly, Crimson is the best colour to use when making up the purples and mauves, but I also needed Cadmium Red because this is better for the oranges.

Each of these six has been mixed with its different neighbouring colour in equal quantities to make the three secondary colours – green, orange and mauve. Next, each of the primaries has been added to the secondaries to create the six tertiary colours, which are made up of about one part secondary and one part primary. Already, as you can see, we have created a veritable rainbow of colours from the two shades of each of the primaries.

Subtler shades   Now comes the fun part! We have fifteen segments. One half of the wheel, the yellows and reds, is the 'warm' half; the other, composed of blues and greens, is the 'cold' half. Colours that lie opposite each other are called 'complementary' colours because, when placed side by side, they immediately intensify or complement each other – the most famous combinations being the trilogy of blue and orange, yellow and mauve, and red and green, much loved by the impressionists in their paintings. The amazing thing is that if, instead of putting opposites side by side, we mix into a segment a small amount of one of its two opposite or complementary colours (since we have fifteen segments) we immediately start to dull or neutralize that colour; add a little more and it will become even more subtle. By adding quite a lot of white to these quieter colours, all sorts of lovely soft pastel shades are obtainable.

Colour experiments   We all know that blue and yellow, mixed in differing proportions, will make all sorts of greens; this range can be vastly expanded by the addition of one or other of the reds. Try just a little at first, then add a little more and see how the colour changes! If it becomes too dirty-looking, add a little more yellow and/or blue. Next, try adding some white to a little of the mixture, then add a bit more white. Each time you alter the colour, paint a dab of it on a piece of white card or paper (keep notes) – in no time at all you will have a veritable wardrobe of greens.

Make your own colour wheel   For a colour-wheel, use acrylic tube paints, putting them on a plate and mixing them with water in the same way as watercolours, but any medium could be used to explore the possibilities. The very best way to learn is to make your own colour wheel and keep it for reference. It could be bigger, with more rings to make room for more variations. Then you could repeat the experiment with emulsions, trying to write against each mixture a rough description of the ingredients that went into it. I frequently find, having made just the colour I want, that I've forgotten to write anything down and, rather like the lost chord, my lovely colour is almost impossible to repeat!

In addition to our four or five tins, we included a brown. All sorts of browns can be made from our existing colours by mixing complementary colours together, but since they involve mixing three colours, it would be difficult to get exactly the same brown each time we mixed it, and brown is the most marvellous colour for dulling all others. This is especially true of the blues and greens on the cold side of the wheel, since browns tend to stem from the opposite or warm side of the wheel, the complementary side to the colds. So by having a separate tin of something like Raw Umber, which is a yellowy brown, we can, for example, add a little to a pale blue to turn it to a lovely Scandinavian blue/grey. Another thing to remember when mixing emulsions is that they always finish up a little darker when dry than they look when wet; put a dab on paper and leave it to dry, then add more white if necessary.

ANTIQUING COLOURS

If your chosen colour appears brighter than you meant it to be once it's painted on and dry, or if it is not quite the right colour, it can always be antiqued, and toned down, or the shade can be altered slightly by then using a glaze over the initial coat.

Glazes are simply transparent films of colour as opposed to an opaque coat. You can use glazes to intensify, neutralize or alter colours, affecting them in the same way as when mixing colours in the colour-wheel, but adding more depth and interest. Plain white, if antiqued with a brown glaze will become a much more pleasing beige or ivory than you could achieve with a solid paint of those colours.

A yellow base coat painted over with either a crimson or blue glaze will become, respectively, either terracotta or green, but both will have the inner glow of the yellow. Dark burgundy-red paint could be a bit oppressive, but it comes to life as a glaze over a lighter red. Equally, if you have painted something yellow and it's not quite right, you will find that an orange or brown glaze will warm it up and make

it more corn-coloured, or a lime-green one will make it more acid.

Sometimes, more than one glaze can give marvellous effects. To achieve a wonderful deep, Scandinavian greeny blue, start with a middle-of-the-road pale blue. Over that, put a Prussian Blue glaze. When dry, follow it with a glaze tinted either with Raw Umber or Green Umber.

If you use oil-tube paint mixed with white spirit, you can wipe it off in places and blend the glaze with paper towel to make it look older. The consistency of the mixture depends on the absorbency of the surface to be painted (*see also page 49*).

I almost never use black with glazes, as it tends to deaden colours, but I sometimes use it when mixing paints rather than glazes; it can be useful in very dark blues or greens, for example, or to dirty up a pink. Amazingly, black with Yellow Ocre and white makes a very good olive green. Other colours for antiquing include browns, such as Burnt Umber and Vandyke Brown.

MATCHING UP

How do you mix a colour to match something, be it a fabric, a carpet, a wallpaper or even a picture in a magazine that includes a colour that you love? What I do is to put the thing I want to match very near the pot I'm using for mixing. Start with a dollop of the nearest colour you possess to the one you want, or mix a colour that is as close to it as you can achieve from the colours that are available. Paint a dab of this on paper beside the colour you are aiming for.

Narrow your eyes a little and flick them from the colour you want to the

colour you've got. Do this several times, almost 'listening' with your eyes, and concentrating hard. Just as you can usually tell when a singer is sharp or flat, you should be able to judge if your colour match needs more of one or other of the primaries – does it need to be warmer or colder, dirtier or cleaner, lighter or darker? If in doubt, a look at the colour wheel should help.

If, after much concentration and mixing you can't quite get it right, go away and leave it for a few hours, coming back to it perhaps first thing the next morning, when the light is good and you are fresh! Never try to mix special colours by electric light, as this dulls and distorts, and try to use no more than three colours and white, plus a neutral, such as brown, grey or black – too many different additions can lead to the dreaded mud colour. This, I am delighted to say, is a problem that is not restricted to you and me, but is even experienced by paint manufacturers!

If at first you don't succeed, do not despair – colour matching is never quick or easy, however often you do it. Because of this, remember always to mix small quantities to begin with, since you don't want to end up with a bucketful of the wrong colour, and write down the quantities as you add them, so that when you get it right you can make lots more.

The bottom half of this selection of colours has been antiqued with a glaze made from Raw Umber oil-tube paint diluted with white spirit to the consistency of tea, painted on sparingly then partly wiped off with paper towel.

DESIGN TECHNIQUES

Before we embark on design techniques, it is important to say that design is not a must. Some things need no embellishment, and others are far better left with just a lovely finish. Just as choosing a colour is a matter of taste, so is the decision whether or not to add a design. I love searching for interesting designs and adapting them to fit the different facets of almost anything and everything, but that doesn't mean you have to share my passion!

Most of the designs we have used are quite simple, based on the tear and comma shapes that have featured in decoration for centuries, with the addition of a few geometrically-based motifs. All are very adaptable; by using a photocopier to enlarge or reduce the trace shapes, their scale can be changed to suit any project. The same applies to the stencils, which can be re-cut, but take care not to make them too small, as a very small stencil can prove difficult to use.

How do we decide which type of design would suit a piece? To start with, most of us have preferences in style; next, whatever your taste you will need inspiration, and there is a wealth of it to be found in libraries and bookshops, card shops and magazines.

Having narrowed down the field, become a doodler – whenever you see a little border or motif that appeals, draw a very rough sketch of it. If you feel you cannot doodle, use a photocopier. When, at a later date, you find just the piece of furniture for it, the copy can be enlarged or reduced, and adpated to either a stencil or tracing.

SCALE AND BALANCE

Now we need to consider the piece of furniture. Where is it going to go? Will it be in light or shade? Should the design be clearly defined or soft; bright or monochromatic? Make a rough drawing of the piece in pencil, large enough to take a doodle of the design, and go over it in ink. Using a pencil, rough out several variations of what you have in mind – if it's a table, you can either divide it in quarters and draw four variations, or use an eraser until you are happy.

This helps you to decide the scale and balance of the design; consider the size of the design in relation to the size of a surface – too small and it will be insignificant and lost, too big and it will not only overpower the piece but probably the room too! The scale needs to be roughly the same for all

facets, large and small, so for the small ones take perhaps only one or two elements from the design used for the larger areas. For example, if a chest of drawers has a 7.5cm (3in) border of flowers and leaves round the top, take just an oval-shaped bunch of them for the centre of each drawer front, aiming for an uneven number, say five or

PLANNING A DESIGN

On the sketch for the bathroom screen, because of their height, each panel was divided into ten sections in order to repeat the freehand design on both end panels. The central design was then made taller, to balance the ends.

seven, but on the same scale as the ones on the top.

Once you are reasonably happy with the format of the design, it is a good idea to measure the item and re-draw it to scale on paper, using a ruler. Divide each facet in four, as with a table top, and sketch the design again. Now, by measuring the scale drawing and multiplying up, you can work out the exact measurements for the real thing. This is particularly important for borders, such as those on the sideboard on *page 72*, which need to fit exactly at the corners.

TRANSFERRING DESIGNS

While making all these plans and doodles, you will probably have selected the base coats or finish for the piece and have prepared and painted it; if not, get it ready now. Next, with scale sketch and ruler in hand, draw the design on the painted surface. The best thing to use for this is blackboard chalk. Using the chalk and ruler, divide each facet in four, just as on the sketch. In effect, you are creating a simple grid system. From this, the centre of each facet and the centre of each of its sides can be found accurately, which is important. Although the chalk lines will be quite wide, they are easy to rub out or alter, whereas pencil marks very often dent the surface and can only be removed with an eraser, which can leave a greasy mark.

Have tracings photocopied to the correct size. If the design has a border, measure its width and, using the chalk, draw two parallel lines round the facet on which it is to go, setting them the measured width apart. Use these as guidelines to keep the border straight. You can either start tracing from the centre of each side, juggling with the corners if necessary, or from the corners outward, leaving a space, if need be, at the centre of each side. Central motifs can be placed accurately over the central chalk cross. Add extra grid lines across and down if you want to position them higher or lower, always measuring with a ruler.

For the tracing, use special purpose-made carbon paper. This comes in several colours, so choose one which will show up on the background. Masking tape can be used for both layers, but easier still is to fix the tracing in place with Blu-tak at the corners. For large designs, cut a piece of carbon to a manageable size and slide it under the tracing, hold it in place and go firmly over

TRACINGS

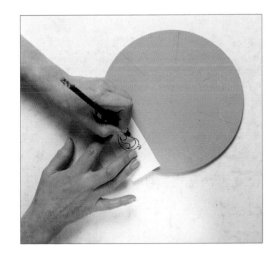

Pencil lines are drawn on an emulsioned tablemat, a protractor and ruler being used to divide it into seven equal segments. Next, the tracing is photocopied to the correct size to fit each segment exactly, forming a border.

the design with a biro or pencil, moving the carbon (not the design) to a new area as necessary.

For a continuous border, trace one section as above, then remove carbon and design, and reposition the design to overlap the end of the first section accurately; secure it; slide the carbon underneath, and repeat the process.

For larger tracings, such as those used for the bathroom on *page 108*, which run to several sheets, roughly cut around the shapes of the design and piece them together accurately on a flat surface, using Blu-tak or masking tape, before fixing them to the project. Again, make sure the design is straight and centred. Use a whole piece of carbon, sliding it under the design from one area to the next.

For stencils such as those used in the breakfast room on *page 84*, draw more chalk lines, at appropriate intervals, to create a closer-knit grid of positioning guidelines (draw a plan on paper first, drawing through the stencils).

FREEHAND EFFECT STENCILS
Stencils, when used on their own, lack fluidity. This is caused by the 'bridges', required to link each section of the design. To achieve a refreshingly different impression, stencils can be used as a guide in one colour, after which you can paint over them and their bridges to give a hand-painted look. If you use white or a pale colour for the initial stencil, it will shine clearly through the subseqent washes of acrylic or watercolour. This obviates the need to add white, which would make those colours opaque as opposed to transparent. By leaving the pale undercolour unpainted for highlights, and using the bridges and some of the edges as a guide for the shadows, you can paint over a stencil, making it look three-dimensional and almost indistinguishable from a free-hand design.

For the example seen overleaf, the leaf swag, drop and flower were first stencilled onto the blue ground with white acrylic primer/undercoat; dip

the stencil brush sparingly into the paint and wipe most of it off on paper towel. Keep the stencil firmly in place with one hand, or attach with masking tape or Blu-tak; hold the brush in an upright position as you apply the paint. When you have finished, remove the stencil, and allow the paint to dry, then paint the branch between the leaves, using a small watercolour or lining brush, and either the same paint or white acrylic tube paint.

In order to make the design appear three-dimensional, like a carving, we have to imagine a light shining across it from one constant direction; by concentrating on one section at a time, we can paint shadows on the sides away from the light, leaving highlights on the edges and curves facing it. Here, the light comes from the top left-hand corner, so the shadows appear under and to the right of each element, while the highlights are left unpainted to the top and left. Since the branch and leaves curve, the placing of the shadows will alter from one leaf to the next as the angle changes.

Using watercolours or acrylic tube paints, start by painting a watery wash over everything except a small highlight to the top/left of each element. Building up the depth of colour from light to dark shades, add a stronger wash to the bridges round the flowers, and to the bottom/right portion of each element, finally putting a stronger or deeper colour, under and to the right of all edges, for the darkest part of the shadows. This will make the whole design look three-dimensional and not at all like a stencil!

BRONZE POWDER STENCILLING
This unusual way of using stencils was popular in the 19th century, especially in America. For this form of stencilling we use small individual stencils of leaves, flowers and fruit, rather than whole sheets of design. The black surface to be stencilled is painted all over with a sparing coat of oil-based varnish to which the bronze

STENCILLING FOR A FREEHAND EFFECT

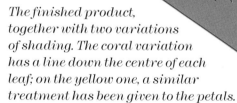

1 Hold the stencil firmly in place; here, white acrylic primer/under-coat is applied over a blue emulsion base. Stencil the swag, then the tails, and finally the flowers, the paint being rubbed on in a circular motion.

2 When the first elements have dried, paint the stalk (the linking element) between the leaves by hand, using a small watercolour or lining brush and the same paint or white acrylic tube paint, mixed with a little water.

The finished product, together with two variations of shading. The coral variation has a line down the centre of each leaf; on the yellow one, a similar treatment has been given to the petals.

3 Imagine the whole stencil is a carving in relief, with a light shining on it from the top left-hand corner; paint a watery wash over it leaving a small, unpainted highlight on the light side of each element.

4 Paint from stalk to leaf tip, gradually adding deeper but narrower washes of colour towards the edges farthest from the imagined light source; these create shadows, the darkest washes being painted at the very edge.

powder will adhere, and this is left for about half an hour until it is partly dry, the exact length of time depending on the varnish used and the surrounding temperature.

Start at the centre of the design with the stencil for one element, such as a single flower or piece of fruit. Place it on the sticky varnish, holding it flat with one hand, and decide where the light might be coming from, in the same way as for the white stencil with washes.

Dip a filbert-shaped fitch brush into a very small amount of gold-bronze powder (which is in fact made from copper and zinc!), taking off the surplus on paper towel. Gently scrub this over the stencil shape, working away from the outer edge which faces the imagined light source, in a circular motion; this will be the strongest gold area. Gradually work towards the shadowy side away from the light, so that less gold will be deposited there,

BRONZE POWDER STENCILLING

1 *Using gold bronze powder, stencil a flower over a still-sticky varnished surface. To make the second flower appear to lie just behind it, overlap the first flower, but apply the powder barely to the edge of the first.*

2 *Add fruit and leaves, putting more gold on the top left-hand side of the design, to indicate the imagined light source. Lastly, stencil an urn, again overlapping it so that it appears to contain the flowers and fruit.*

3 *For a shaded border, start with the topmost leaf; overlap the stencil in the identical place for each subsequent leaf, applying powder sparingly just to the tips and edges, and leaving the centres dark.*

until there is almost none in the darkest shadows. Add a little more powder to the lightest parts if necessary, always taking great care that it doesn't flick or drift onto the surrounding sticky surface. To avoid this, move the brush very slowly!

Now, carefully and slowly lift up the stencil; try to keep it horizontal until it is clear of the surface, as it may have specks of gold on it which can drift onto the varnish. Wipe the stencil clean and replace it, or another stencil, next to or overlapping the original flower.

If you are overlapping the first shape, the idea is to make this second one look as though it lies behind the first, so this time, use the same method, but don't go over the first shape, the darkest part between them forming more shadows. Continue like this, outwards, ending either with a mixture of outer leaves, gold at their

edges and darker in the centre, to set the whole design off or, as in this example, a container in the form of an urn, or indeed both leaves and container.

Allow at least twelve hours for the oil-based varnish to dry before fixing the bronze powder with an oil-based spray varnish. (If one uses a brush at this stage, the powder left on the surface will smear.) When the spray coat is dry, it should be safe to brush on a coat of oil-based varnish.

If you have decided to add a line around a piece to make it look more striking, or perhaps around just one section, such as a drawer front, paint this first. It is not difficult to paint lines (*see overleaf*); don't panic if the line is not absolutely straight – we want it to look hand-painted, not machine made! When the piece is finished, one looks at the overall effect, not at the one

bit of line or brush stroke that went slightly awry. Such minor errors will, if anything, add to its charm.

MATCHING AND ADAPTING
Sometimes you may want to adapt a fabric or wallpaper design. Doodles are the answer; you will not want to repeat the whole design, probably just elements. The doodles will show you what will work and which are the easiest elements to adapt (these usually prove the most effective).

If the fabric or paper has a simple border, this is ideal, but you may find the border too fiddly, as I did with the fabric in the picture on *page 107*. For the bedhead there, I used the same colours as the roses in the fabric, but painted them on a smaller scale and in my own style, concentrating on the leaves of the fabric design to join the two together.

BRUSHSTROKES

Children like to draw houses, trees, flowers and people with a pencil and then, with a small brush, paint them in, using lots of little brushstrokes with the aim of making the colour as solid as possible, with no visible brushmarks. They will go over the painting a second and even a third time, to ensure that no paper shows through.

If we were to use the same technique on furniture, the design would tend to be static, lacking spontaneity and flow, and it would take a very long time to paint! To help us to avoid these pitfalls, there is a selection of brushes, each a particular length and shape, and designed for a specific purpose, enabling us in one brushstroke to create a leaf or bud, petal or ribbon, full of light, shade and movement. Standard watercolour brushes, which are called 'round', come in several different bristle lengths. The medium ones are good all-purpose brushes, but for stems and lines it is much easier to use a brush with a longer bristle (in general, the longer the line, the longer the bristle needed to paint it); on the other hand, a shorter bristle helps to give a perfect shape to a stubby petal, in one stroke.

PAINTING LINES

Straight lines (perhaps curving around corners) are very often used as a finishing touch, to emphasize or enclose a design. Painting a straight freehand line can be a daunting proposition and the comment about children applies here also – the lines must flow, without obvious stops and starts and the mistakes that this may cause.

If you like, you can rest your hand against a length of picture-frame moulding, with the raised edge turned in towards the intended line, and use this as a guide. The key to success when painting lines, either with a guide or freehand, however, is to use the correct brush, known as a 'coachliner' or 'stripper'. The hairs of a coachliner are all the same length, to keep the painted line the same thickness, and brushes are available in lengths ranging from 1.5cm (½in), used for short straight lines and small curves, to 5cm (2in), which is used for long straight lines.

To use a coachliner, start by making a puddle of paint large enough to cover the full length of the hairs. The paint might be either a coloured acrylic tube paint, bound with a little white paint mixed with water, or an emulsion diluted with water to a creamy consistency. Moisten the brush with water, then lay the hairs in the paint, drawing the brush towards you; turn the brush over and repeat the process until the hairs are saturated with paint and the brush is completely filled up to the ferrule (the metal join), rather like a fountain pen filled with ink.

LONG LINES

To paint a long line, on a piece of furniture, for example, stand with one foot about a pace behind the other, as near

---

LONG LINES

When using a lining brush, ensure the bristles are filled with paint and hold the brush like a pen; move it with your whole body rather than your hand, leaning forwards then shifting your weight back as you paint.

---

as possible to the point at which the line is to finish. Rest your weight on your front foot, leaning forwards and stretching out to the start of the line. Either hold the brush like a pen or cradle it in your upturned hand, with your thumb on top to steady it, and your knuckles touching the surface to guide you. Place the tip of the brush in one corner, a little way in from the edge and the same distance down from the corner (the edges of the furniture can make useful visual guidelines). Gently lower the brush down in a straight line, until two thirds lie on the surface, then gradually move your weight from the front foot to the back, drawing the brush with you. As you reach the end, slowly start to raise the brush, finishing by lifting the tip of the brush away at the end of the line.

If you have to reload the brush in the middle of a long line, overlap the end of the previous brush stroke. Keep a damp cloth handy for minor corrections.

SHORT LINES

For shorter lines, about 20–30cm (8–10in) long, you can sit down. For lines under 20cm (8in) and small curves, use a shorter coachliner. You may find it helpful to make a light pencil or chalk guideline for curves. When all the lines are dry, you can correct wobbles and add definition, by going over them a second time.

LONG TEAR-SHAPED LEAVES

1 Load the brush and press the whole length of the bristles firmly down at the start of the stroke; without lifting, slur them slightly sideways, away from the intended direction of the curve, to fatten the end.

2 Moving your whole hand, start the curve; gradually lift the bristles, causing the stroke to get narrower, while keeping the handle at the same angle to the surface, and in line with the curve.

3 Two thirds of the way through the stroke, while still lifting, roll the top of the brush a quarter of the way around towards the inside of the curve to bring it onto the pointed edge, lifting it off as that point is reached.

TEAR SHAPES

When I first started painting on furniture, my search for designs led me to hunt through books on folk art from all over the world, and to study porcelain and pottery designs, painted eggs and traditional barge painting. In all the cultures, whether ancient or modern, I found one resounding common denominator – a shape like a tear drop or a comma. Curved and straight variations of this brushstroke have been used for centuries in decoration, from ancient Etruscan art to Rosemaling in Norway, each culture adapting it to suit their taste and style, borders and centrepieces being formed from various sizes of it. Because of its adaptability, I determined to master the tear drop, and I suggest you do the same – it is invaluable.

Using a round watercolour brush, lie the length of the bristles into a creamy mixture of your chosen medium. Zigzag it in the paint, turning the brush

SHORT TEAR-SHAPED LEAVES

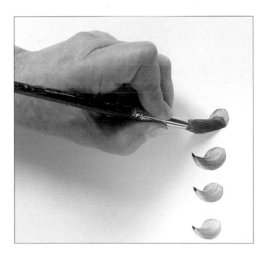 

1 This time, press only about one third of the bristles down and slur them sideways, away from the direction in which you want the curve to go, before starting to move around it, gradually lifting the brush.

2 Keep the handle in line with the direction of the curve, lifting the brush to narrow the bristles, and rolling them in towards the centre, as in step 3 above, before lifting the point away, to leave a tidy 'tail'.

over to ensure that it is well loaded. Lay the tip, followed by the whole length of the bristles, at the place where you want the stroke to start. Press down firmly, which will splay the bristles; slur them sideways away from the direction of the curve just a little, still pressing the whole brush to the surface. This will give the stroke its nice fat beginning.

Start to move the brush in the direction of the curve, gradually easing the pressure and beginning to lift the bristles up. This will cause them to start coming together again, narrowing the breadth of the stroke in preparation for the tidy pointed end. Three quarters of the way through the stroke when only about a third of the bristles are still on the surface, twist the top of the brush in towards the curve, while still lifting and travelling; the twist must not be more than a quarter

round in order for the tip of the brush to finish at the sharp edge caused by the original splaying of the bristles at the beginning of the stroke.

You will also notice from the photographs that the angle of the handle to the surface does not change, this means that your whole hand must move; the wrist not remaining at the starting place. Also, at the beginning of the stroke, the handle of the brush should be in line with the tip of the bristles. As the stroke moves round the curve, the end of the handle should lead the way so that when the bristles are taken off, it is then in a straight line with the take-off point.

This stroke can be used in many ways: for folk-art leaves, of course, daisy petals, and all sorts of acanthus-type scroll designs, such as the tracings on the sideboard (*see page 72*), the kitchen chair (*page 84*), and the waste-

bin and lampshade in the study (*page 60*). By using just the tip of the same brush, but without pressing down the full length of the bristles to begin with, it is possible to make shorter, fatter versions of the tear drop, ideal for rose petals, or two touching each other, for the primrose family and violets, though you will find that these are even easier to execute if you use a shorter-bristled round brush.

If you want to paint a straight tear instead of a curved one, the same principles apply, except in the twist towards the end. This can be in whichever direction is most comfortable, but you should still take care not to twist the brush more than a quarter of the way round in order to lift the brush away at the point where the bristles are at their sharpest edge.

It is worth practising these strokes, and in all directions, before starting on

STRAP-SHAPED LEAVES

1 Start defining a flattened S shape with the tip of the brush; gradually press the bristles down, and travel sideways until you reach the middle of the S, keeping the handle in line with the starting point.

2 From the middle onwards, start lifting the bristles and continue around the second curve of the S. The brush will deposit more intense colour as the stroke continues to narrow, giving shading to the shape.

3 Towards the end of the stroke, roll the brush in a quarter of the way round towards the centre of the curve again, to reach and take off at the knife-edge of the bristles that is produced by the pressure in the middle.

a project. As with learning to ride a bicycle, it doesn't always come easily, but once you've got the knack, you've got it forever!

S SHAPES

Having mastered the tear drop, we are going to add a bit to the beginning of it for an S-shaped 'strap' stroke, ending with the same little twist as before. Put the very tip of the brush on the surface and, moving it in the shape of a flattened S, press down gradually to the middle of the stroke; from here, it becomes the same as the long tear drop, so lift the brush as you move through the second half of the S shape, twisting inwards and taking it off the surface. This time, note that while the handle still stays at the same angle to the surface throughout, so that the whole hand is again moving with the stroke, the end of the handle keeps pointing more or less in the same direction from beginning to end.

This stroke can be mixed with tear shapes to make scrolls and is also very useful for twining ribbons.

The first stroke of a two-stroke leaf shape is a mixture of the two; this is ideal for rose leaves, or you can use lots of small ones for freehand leaf swags, like those in our stencil on *page 88*. With the brush almost at right angles to the direction in which you are going, put the brush tip on the branch, and moving towards the leaf tip, push the bristles towards the branch and move out sideways. Because the bristles are almost at right angles, the start of the stroke will be nearly as wide as a leaf. Begin to lift, reducing the width, and this time twist the top of the brush away from the original curve, out rather than in, forming a miniature 's'. The second stroke starts in the same way, but make it curve the other way, ending with a little twist in towards the centre of the imaginary circle. The two together will give the leaf highlights and realistic shadows down the centre and at the edges, with no further titivating needed!

DOUBLE STROKED LEAVES

1 With the brush almost at right angles to the painted stalk, press about one third of the bristles down and travel sideways towards the tip of the leaf, curving the stroke slightly round yourself.

2 Lift the bristles to narrow the stroke, rolling the tip of the brush away from you just before taking it off the surface, making the end of the stroke curve in towards the branch, depositing the paint in a shadowed effect.

3 To broaden the leaf, add a second stroke parallel to the first, not pressing down quite so much at the beginning and imagining the stroke curving away from you, towards the tip of the leaf.

4 Once more, lift the bristles as you go to narrow the stroke. Follow the original curve, twisting the tip of the brush away from you again at the end, a quarter of the way round, before taking it off the surface.

BOWS

Bows like crumpled silk with dancing tails are really a conglomeration of all the brushstrokes. While keeping the brush on the move, first press the length of it down, then lift it up so that only the tip skims the surface. Do this at erratic inteyals while fidgeting it in an irregular zigzag, keeping it moving all the time for a wonderful imitation of a twisting ribbon.

PAINTING BOWS

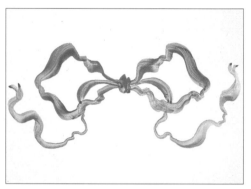

Imagine a kite shape for each side of the bow; paint the knot first, then, alternately pressing and lifting, wobble the brush from the knot around the kite. Add the tails in the same manner.

ROSES

For my beloved roses, we need to understand the principles of light and shade, since this stylized image relies heavily on their use. First of all we have to establish in our minds from which direction the light source is coming; here, let's choose the top left-hand corner. Whichever way any element in a design is facing, the direction of the light will remain constant, so with the light in this position, the shadows will be from east to south and the highlights from north to west.

Draw a ball in pencil or blackboard chalk and decide where the rose is facing. Unless it is looking straight at us, its centre will not be in the middle of the ball, but nearer to the side at which

it is facing. The reason for this is that, in perspective, the further something is from the eye, the smaller and narrower it becomes. Put a pencil or chalk mark for the centre. Paint the ball, trying to apply the paint as you would if asked to paint the latitude lines on a globe, with increasing circles radiating from that central point (imagining this to be the south pole). While it is still wet, use the original colour to mix a darker shade and fill in the centre, followed by shadows round the side furthest from the light, still imitating lines of latitude. Then, with the same deeper colour, and using the short tear-shaped stroke, paint petals round the ball on the opposite side to the shadows, starting with the foreshortened smallest one on the arc nearest the centre of the rose, and overlapping

them slightly as you come round to the base, each one getting a little larger because of the perspective.

Stop when you reach the beginning of the shadow on the ball, and mix some white into your original colour. Stroke it round the side of the ball which faces the light, latitudinally as before, leaving a little of the original middle tone if possible. With the same lighter-coloured paint on the brush, paint the paler petals, starting next to the one you first painted and working your way round to the base of the rose. When the rest of the design has been painted and all is dry, you can go back and adjust the highlights and shadows a little if need be, making the lightest parts a little lighter, and the deep shadows darker; don't over-do it, as too much contrast makes roses harsh.

PAINTING A ROSE

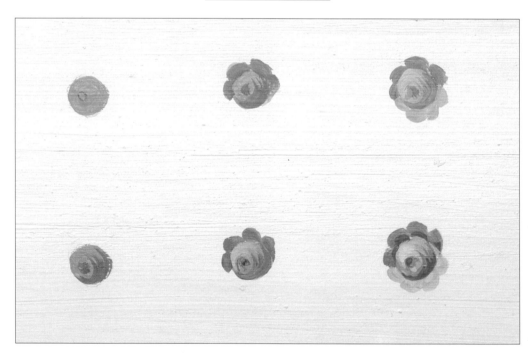

Using a light-to-middle tone, paint a ball, with brushstrokes circling the centre. Next, add a deeper tone for the shadows and, with the same colour, the darker petals, starting from the top of the rose. Add white to the original colour to highlight the ball and paint the petals on the shady side of it. When this has dried, emphasize the darks and lights a little more.

CHOOSING A MEDIUM

When deciding which medium to use, first imagine how you want it to look when it's finished. This is not just a question of choosing the colour, whether dark or pastel, but of deciding whether it should look solid and opaque, or washy and transparent, and choosing the appropriate medium and technique.

Each medium has its own individual qualities, and you have at least five different types of tube paint from which to choose, as well as the possibility of using emulsions, stencil paints or enamels. Add to these the options of negative-image designs, such as penwork, in which the background is painted round the design, or designs that are gilded, using leaf, plus the special paints for porcelain and fabrics, and we have a very wide choice.

WATERCOLOURS

When taking a holiday, my greatest pleasure is to indulge in another form of painting, watercolour landscape – weather permitting! It is only fairly recently that I experimented with watercolours on furniture, as I had always supposed that since they are so vulnerable to rain or damp, they would not be varnishable. My experiment, to my amazement, proved that I had been wrong; so long as only an oil glaze or varnish or a spirit-based lacquer is put on top, rather than anything water-based, the watercolour not only stays intact but is also waterproof from then on.

This means that you can create lovely soft designs by painting with watercolours on surfaces similar to watercolour paper, such as matt emulsion or any of the softer chalkier paints, and watercolours are also ideal for shading over pale stencils.

Because pure watercolour will not stick to an oil-based surface, or to one that has a sheen – a silk vinyl, for example, or glossy metal paint – it is not possible to use it for projects where base coats of this type have been used.

Unlike acrylic paints, watercolours have the added advantage that you can blend them into each other, and wipe off colour, perhaps to create highlights or if one part looks too heavy. Because of their transparency, they would not work well over a darkish base, but over white or a pale shade, the light shines through them in a way that would be difficult to achieve with any of the other mediums.

ACRYLIC TUBE PAINTS

Acrylic tube paints are extremely versatile, and we tend to use these more than any other medium.

They are unlike watercolours in that they are happy to cling to shiny surfaces, such as silk vinyl, cellulose metal paint, or shellac-based lacquers. If you are using acrylics over oil-based eggshell or gloss, you may need to key the surface by wiping it with a damp sponge dipped in fullers' earth or talcum. Alternatively, use a damp nylon pan scrubber! When painting acrylics over glossy or oil-based surfaces, it is best not to add too much water, but over matt emulsion or softer paints, you can add lots of water to acrylics

EFFECTS OF DIFFERENT MEDIUMS

Paints can change the look of a design; from the left, we have two watercolour scrolls, two in acrylics (the first without white, the second with), two more in acrylics mixed with glaze, and two in oils, the second with added white.

and they will resemble watercolours, though they cannot be blended when dry.

They can also be mixed with acrylic medium or varnish for a thicker, but still transparent, glaze effect, added to acrylic paste to give a textured design, or simply used straight from the tube with a very little water, to resemble oils. Because they dry within fifteen to twenty minutes, the danger of smudging is reduced, and being waterproof when dry, no amount of antiquing or varnishing of any sort will disturb them. Some waxes, however, can dissolve acrylic paints, so if you are waxing it is safest to varnish first with water- or oil-based varnish.

DESIGNER'S GOUACHE

Designer's gouache is another water-based paint which, like watercolour, is not waterproof, being bound with the same medium, gum arabic. The main difference between this and the two previous types, is that it is less transparent, having a proportion of chalky filler in it; this makes it useful where a blended opaque look is needed as opposed to the transparency of water-colour. Being water-soluble when dry, it is less manageable for designs than acrylics, but the colours, when mixed with acrylic scumble or varnish, become waterproof and are stronger in tone than acrylic tube colours.

Gouache is also reluctant to cling to a glossy surface, except a shellac-based one, but it is very good for designs in which opaque colours need to be blended when dry; for example, when painting imaginary moulding or panelling with shading and highlights. When used over a barrier such as sanding sealer, it is the easiest of mediums to remove if one goes wrong! Because of this, remember only to use oil-based varnish over gouache, as a water-based varnish would remove it.

OILS AND ALKYDS

Oils are wonderfully malleable, but take a long time to dry. What is more, some colours take longer to dry than others, which means that after a week, when you think your design is dry enough to varnish, horror of horrors, one colour runs! To avoid this pitfall, use alkyd paints. These are also soluble in white spirit, but they all dry at the same speed, much more quickly than oils. Instead of linseed oil, they are bound by a manmade oil or resin called alkyd, and once dry will safely accept oil-, water- or spirit-based substances. Both oils and alkyds will happily go over any base coat, glossy or matt, water-, oil- or spirit-based.

Added to the possibilities described above, you also have the interesting options of using penwork for negative designs and goldleaf, as shown below.

PENWORK

An outline is drawn with a waterproof pen, and shadows are then hatched in. Next, the shadows are crosshatched and the first coat of backgound painted in. To finish, a second background coat of black emphasizes the design. A coat of water-based varnish will protect the ink from subsequent finishes.

GOLD LEAF

To use gold leaf, first paint the shape in goldsize, then apply transfer leaf and remove the backing. Smooth over the leaf with a soft brush or cotton wool, leaving loose pieces to be cleaned off when dry; the motif is sealed with spirit-based lacquer, then shaded with Burnt Umber acrylic paint.

FINISHING

The final stage of painting any piece of furniture involves at least one coat of varnish or wax, but for a really beautiful finish we can do more than that. In fact, the finishing stage is almost as important as the preparation, as it can change the whole appearance of a piece.

If you have applied a design, this could now be carefully distressed, using fine sandpaper. The piece can be antiqued in various ways, including crackle varnishing. After this, you can choose which kind of varnish to use, how many coats to apply, and whether or not to end with waxing.

ANTIQUING

Before embarking on antiquing, give everything a coat of plain water-based varnish. This will prevent the 'patina' sinking in, but it will enable you to remove some or all of of the antiquing if you are unhappy with the result.

The easiest way to antique is to mix oil-tube paint with white spirit to the correct consistency for the absorbency of the surface over which it is to be painted. This can range from a consistency of tea over a matt surface, such as emulsion, to thin cream over a mid-sheen one, such as silk vinyl or eggshell. Paint the mixture all over the piece, a facet at a time; leave it for a few seconds, minutes or more, depending on how strong an effect you want, then remove the surplus with a cloth or paper towel, streaking it off in the direction of the grain of the wood.

If you have painted a design in thickish paint or the base coats have brush marks in them, an extra option is to allow the oil paint to half dry for a few minutes after wiping off, then stroke over the design or across the brushmarks with the flats of your fingers. This drives the antiquing into all the dips and brushmarks while removing it from the peaks in a way unachievable with the paper towel.

If the effect is too dark when finished, more can be removed by wiping with a paper towel moistened with a little white spirit. If you need to slow the drying process in order to have longer to blend it, you can add a little linseed oil or oil-based scumble glaze to the mixture.

The colours for antiquing vary depending on the effect you want and the tone of the base coat. The most useful colour is Raw Umber, the colour of old dust! For a more yellow aged look, such as the colour seen on the chest of drawers in the bedroom, which resembles the colour of ancient varnish, Raw Sienna can be added to Raw Umber (half and half). Over darker colours, a deeper, warmer brown such as Burnt Umber or Vandyke Brown may be needed; if the base is very dark, you can add a little black.

To antique pale blues, Green Umber, much used in Scandinavia, will give a dirty, more turquoise effect than Raw Umber, while Burnt Sienna, a strong brick colour, looks wonderful over yellows, intensifying them, but when put over blues, it will dull and neutralize them. Another very useful colour is Payne's Grey, which is a lovely blue grey – the colour of the sea on a dull day. This is very good over the warmth of off-whites and beiges, giving an old ivory shade, and it is equally effective over pale blues and greens. You can use water-based glaze, but this dries more quickly than oils, leaving less time for playing with the glaze and making adjustments. For an ageing coat that you can leave in place, tint water-based varnish with brown acrylic tube paint or the stronger-coloured gouaches. Some manufacturers make good stains to mix with their acrylic varnishes, and these are ideal (*see suppliers list, page 126*). If it ends up too dark or has too many brushmarks, remember that the solvent for all acrylics is methylated spirits, so you can put a little on a cloth and soften the colour when dry.

Alternatively, paint on a coat of shellac, brushing sparingly and streakily in the direction of the grain. Its orange brown tones colours down; since it dries so quickly, give the piece a coat of satin water-based varnish first, and allow it to dry thoroughly.

VARNISHING

Whether you have antiqued your project or not, in general it is sensible to protect it with varnish; the type and the number of coats largely depends on the end use. Common sense usually dictates whether an item needs just one coat or lots. None of the varnishes, whether water- or oil-based, are completely heat proof, but most are heat resistant and in general waterproof, whereas the spirit-based lacquers are not, but can be coated with varnishes to protect them.

Only varnish in daylight, and apply it in manageable sections, working each new section back into the last a little. Don't wear fluffy clothes, and never attempt to go back to a half dry bit to remove a dog hair or smooth it – wait till it is dry. Each coat should be completely dry and, ideally, very lightly sanded and the dust wiped off with a tak-rag before the next coat is applied.

WAXING

After a top coat of matt or satin has cured for two weeks, you can add to its antique lustre by waxing, either with plain furniture wax, or with tinted or stained waxes which darken the surface, making it look even older.

Part Two

PROJECTS

This section contains a range of projects illustrated with step-by-step photographs demonstrating the techniques explained earlier, together with other examples of finished items. The stencils and trace-offs included with this book have been used on the projects, but these only indicate one possible use for each design, and I hope that you will enjoy adapting them to your own individual needs and taste. When buying items of furniture to be decorated, remember that it is the bone structure that matters; as long as the shape is attractive, the most shiny finish or unfashionable colour scheme will be forgotten by the time you have worked your transformation!

The SITTING ROOM

My sitting room was a near disaster because it has no chimney! To me, a fireplace is not just a source of warmth and comfort, but a focal point, and the most important part of any room where one is to relax. What could I do? The words of one of my greatest friends rang in my ears: 'Any fool can be uncomfortable'. Read it how you will, it is a marvellous phrase, defying defeat! It was not possible to put in a flue, so I could not even have a pretty gas coal or log fire. Only electricity was left, and although the resulting fireplace is not quite what I wanted, it is infinitely better than no fire at all.

Even when the sun is out this room can be quite dark, so strong jewel colours have been used to make it more cosy, with lots of coral to provide warmth. The colours for the marbles on the table were chosen by picking them from the painting above the mantelpiece, a Florentine scene which also adds a sense of Mediterranean warmth to the room. The shape of the table top itself was inspired by the wastepaper bin on page 58. The curves of the bin sides, adapted to fit six times into a circle, evolved into this very elegant shape, which was just the right size to fit the topless pedestal that had been waiting for years in the loft!

A MARBLEIZED WINE TABLE

MATERIALS
*Paints etc: selection of base
colours in vinyl silk or
matt emulsion, satin
water-based varnish,
acrylic scumble glaze,
gouache or acrylic tubes
for tinting (here, Burnt
Umber, Burnt Sienna,
Ultramarine, crimson,
white and Veridian),
methylated spirits, and
oil-based varnish.*

*Brushes: Badger
softener, 12mm (½in)
decorator's, watercolour
(small, long), varnish and
short lining brushes, plus
a feather and a cloth.*

The wine table is made from medium density fibreboard (MDF); this is a wonderful material on which to paint, and when cut it also gives neat tidy edges, which need very little sanding to make them smooth. There are many ways in which this table could have been treated, but its shape, and the bright colours used throughout the room, made the temptation of marbleizing in panels irresistible. For this reason, we chose quite a thick board, to give a good paintable edge, making the marble look more convincing.

For ease of painting, the top was painted first and then attached to the base. The first, sealing, coat was acrylic primer/undercoat. When dry, this was lightly sanded to smooth the surface, which tends to rise a little when a water-based paint is applied.

For a varied pattern of this nature, start by planning the size and arrangement of the marble panels on paper, then use a ruler and pencil (chalk would not show on white primer) to measure and draw the lines for the panels on the actual object. The simplest way to draw the outer edge is by measuring in and marking and then joining pencil dots; if some of the curves look distorted, you can adjust them a little.

Make a series of test colours with glazes over them to find the right combinations to create your marble effects. Be sure to keep an exact record of each combination. Next, paint the panels with the selection of emulsion base coats you have chosen, and then coat the table with a satin water-based varnish. This gives a mid-sheen finish to the surface, enabling the subsequent glazes to be softened and moved around.

Marbleize the masked panels in your chosen colours, following the technique on *page 28*. Remove the tape after you have completed each panel, and allow the first group of panels (*see step 6*) to dry at least overnight. You can speed up the process in front of a fire or radiator, but don't leave the table too close!

Rather than masking again, give the whole surface another coat of satin water-based varnish. When this is dry, you will be able to marbleize the remaining panels freely, tidying up the edges with paper towel where they have overlapped the dry panels. Once they too are dry, apply another coat of satin water-based varnish, then choose whether or not to mask the outer curved panels, as shown in *step 7*.

After lining the panels with acrylic tube paint (*see step 8*), apply one or two coats of water-based satin or gloss varnish (perhaps more than two, if only water-based varnish is to be used). Sand lightly before the final coat. Alternatively, finish with one or two coats of oil-based varnish, sanding lightly before the final coat to make the surface as smooth and marble-like as possible.

1 Draw the panel outlines with a ruler and
pencil. For outer panels, measure in with
the ruler at right angles to the edge every 2cm
(³/₄in) or so, putting in pencil dots. If the curve
looks out of line with the outer edge, adjust
accordingly. Join the dots by eye.

2 Paint each of the panels with the appropriate colour of base coat, using either silk
vinyl on its own or matt emulsion, which
should be followed when dry by a coat of satin
water-based varnish, to give it a sheen. Allow
to dry thoroughly.

3 Lay masking tape lightly along every
other panel to contain the glaze within the
outline, only pressing it flat at the very edge,
and first laying each strip two or three times
on cotton clothing, to reduce the stickiness and
prevent it removing the undercoat.

4 Apply drifts of coloured acrylic glaze tinted with gouache (see page 28). For this
panel, the glazes were mixed with Burnt
Umber, crimson and white. Remove the surplus by patting with stockinette, then soften
lightly in all directions with the badger brush.

You can create a carved
effect on marble by
painting on a design
using shadows and
highlights.

5 After softening in all directions, add negative veins by using methylated spirits on a small brush, opening up the glaze back to the paler base coat. For light veins, use white gouache mixed with water, tracing them very lightly with a small brush.

6 Soften the white veins in all directions, making them appear to sink into the surface. When every alternate panel is complete, remove the tape and allow to dry; coat the surface with satin water-based varnish, then marbleize the panels between.

RIGHT. Here you can see how the glaze and veins have been taken over the edges, to give the impression of thick marble. Veins are like rifts through the surface, and are angled downwards when viewed in cross-section from the side. The pedestal was painted with the khaki green base colour used on the top. The same Veridian Green glaze, mixed with a little Burnt Umber, that was used for both shades of the green marble was then dragged over the pedestal, to complement the marbles without overpowering them. When all was dry, several coats of water-based varnish were applied, followed by two or three of oil-based varnish. The table was sanded lightly after the water-based coats and between the oil-based ones, to give a marble-like finish.

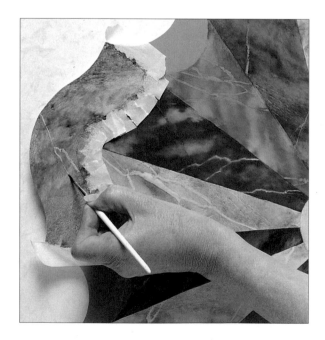

7 For the outer panels, either varnish again before marbleizing or mask the curve with torn pieces of tape; take the glaze down over the edge, following the thickness of the marble. Here Veridian Green glaze was used, with Burnt Umber added for the darkest areas.

8 When all is dry, use a small lining brush to paint a line between all the panels, to define them and obliterate any wobbly edges. The darkest red of the marbleizing colours was used here – a mixture of crimson and Burnt Umber, plus a little white.

LEFT. The MDF mantelpiece was first sealed with shellac, then rubbed with a candle (see page 19); this was followed by acrylic primer/undercoat, distressed with medium sandpaper when dry. The MDF was then streaked in the direction of the imaginary grain with water-based varnish tinted with Raw Umber acrylic tube paint. The mouldings were picked out with two coats of the undercoat, and the whole surface was finally sealed with two coats of the varnish, untinted.

Behind the fire is a sheet of MDF, marbleized to match the table. This was worked in manageable sections; a wet edge of un-marbled glaze was left between sections, to enable the next section to be blended in.

The picture frame was an old damaged one. It was left in a rainy garden for a week, then stripped back to the wood and re-gilded (see page 33). After this, it was verdigrised, except for the middle section. Here, the leaf was distressed with fine wire wool, and the design was applied with water-based size and leaf.

ABOVE. The same Veridian-tinted acrylic scumble was used for both the lamp and the clock, but after an initial coat of acrylic primer/undercoat the emulsion base coat colours varied. For the lamp, which was white gloss rubbed down with sandpaper, the khaki and pale turquoise of the table's green panels was used; for the clock, which was oak and was also sanded, a paler turquoise was used. When each was dry, satin water-based varnish was applied for a mid-sheen surface.

The glaze used for the lamp was applied in sections from the base up, each one being bagged immediately with a thin crumpled plastic bag (see page 26). The glaze for the clock was dragged on the front, in a circular motion to echo the dial. When the glaze was dry, water-based goldsize was applied to the spiral uprights and the clock mouldings. These were then gilded with Dutch metal leaf, and antiqued a little with Raw Umber emulsion (see page 49). Both the clock and the lamp were sealed with water-based varnish.

The
STUDY

A study, being the room where one works and creates, needs to have a sense of energy – the sort of energy that greets you when you walk into it in the morning, stimulating you to do greater things than ever before. The most stimulating of all colours is red. I would not choose red for many rooms, and it should always be used in moderation but, as you can see, the red of the mantelpiece, lamp and bin, and red uniform in the painting immediately raise the spirits, rather like taking a deep refreshing breath.

Used to extremes, red can be overpowering, so to balance the energy it produces, a cool turquoise blue has been used for the walls and the rest of the furniture, with a softer version of the red echoed in the design on the desk. Because the mantelpiece is such a strong colour, the frame of the painting over it needed equally bold treatment if it were not to appear insipid in contrast, so we have created a thoroughly ornate frame. The design for this was inspired by an eighteenth-century one seen at Osterley Park years ago. The Osterley frame, which is beautifully handcarved, has gilded scrolls on a cream background. Here, we have matched the background to the colour of the collar in the portrait, but any colour could look just as striking, and the frame, of course, could be larger or much smaller, to suit your purpose.

A GILDED PICTURE FRAME

The wonderful gentleman in the portrait was painted by my mother, but was never framed. Wanting something really large and ornate, I decided to create a frame from MDF and a selection of mouldings (see suppliers' list). Having measured the picture and the chosen mouldings, the frame was planned on paper to suit these measurements; it was then cut to size and made up by a local joiner.

If you are making your own frame, you will need to cut the straight mouldings for the edges of the frame to length using a mitre-box for the corners. It is not particularly easy to do this, and you may prefer to have the mitred ends cut professionally. Use a contact adhesive to secure the mitred strips (very heavy pieces may need to be pinned as well).

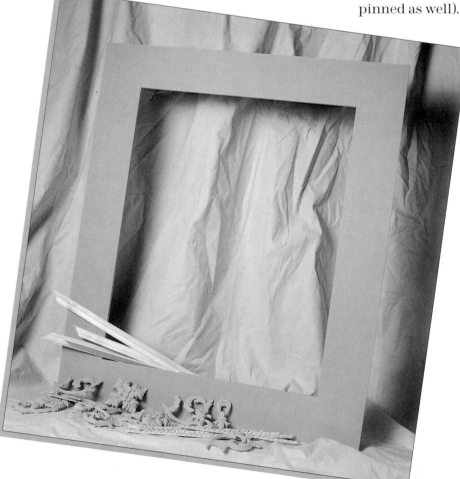

When positioning the decorative mouldings (see step 1), it helps if you mark the centre of the frame on each side, so that you can position the pieces evenly. Apply the adhesive to the marked outline on the frame and to the back of each moulding, a side at a time, attaching them after between ten and fifteen minutes.

The mouldings used here are of 'composition', which is stronger than plastic. It is possible to find either wooden ones, or bendable types which are made of softer material and are ideal for applying to a shaped end or curved surface. Even plastic mouldings, once they have been sealed with shellac and painted or gilded, can look wonderful. Plaster mouldings can also be gilded; remember to moisten them with water before applying the shellac, and follow this by a coloured emulsion – browny red, black, or Yellow Ochre.

For silver or aluminium leaf, use black, Raw Umber or deep blue as an undercolour. If left unsealed, silver leaf will gradually mellow and oxidize, wheras aluminium will not. Raw Umber, used over either of these to antique it, will give a silver-gilt or steel appearance.

The patinating fluid (see page 34) is applied on top of the Dutch metal leaf used for this frame to age its appearance. Use upholstery cotton or cotton wool, soaking it well and wearing rubber gloves. You can achieve this effect with vinegar, but it can take up to twelve hours to work. Pat the liquid on a section at a time, aiming mainly for the flat background, drying it off with paper towel as it begins to darken; for a darker effect, repeat the process and dry again.

When antiquing the raised mouldings (see step 8), cover only some 5-7.5cm (2-3in) at a time. You can use Raw Umber acrylic tube paint instead of the dark brown emulsion used here, but whichever you use, make sure it goes into all the indentations, wiping it off the highlights immediately with paper towel, to leave the crevices looking antique.

1 Cut each end of the straight frame sections at an angle of 45°. Attach the mitred pieces with contact adhesive, and coat the surface with shellac. Arrange and draw round the curly mouldings with pencil, then secure them in place with contact adhesive.

2 Coat the curly mouldings with shellac, applying it sparingly, but making sure it goes into all the indentations. When this has dried, paint the whole surface of the frame with brownish-red emulsion, ensuring it is not applied too thickly in the dips.

3 When the emulsion is dry, give the whole frame a sparing coat of water-based gold-size. This looks milky when applied, but dries to a transparent shine in about fifteen minutes, by which time it is at the correct stage of tackiness for the leaf to be laid.

4 Cut the transfer Dutch metal leaf to fit each section; starting with the straight borders, lay each piece so that it overlaps the last a little. Fill in the centre, using smaller pieces and pressing the leaf into the mouldings with your fingers as much as possible.

If you do not wish to use mouldings, you can trace the above design on to your frame and paint it.

5 Inevitably, there will be small gaps where the leaf cannot reach; cover these by dabbing over them with a fitch dipped in matching gold bronze powder; smooth all over the leaf with cotton wool or a soft brush. If there are still gaps, reapply the size to them and patch.

6 Leave overnight to dry, then remove all loose bits with a soft brush or cotton wool. To age the frame, moisten cotton wool or wadding with patinating fluid, dabbing it over the flat part of the surface, and drying with paper towel when dark enough.

RIGHT. To finish the ageing process, the outer border of the frame is rubbed along its length with fine wire wool, revealing some of the base colour. The wire wool makes the water-based size beneath the leaf appear grey. To remove this, wipe gently with white spirit on a paper towel. When you are happy with the overall effect, gild the outer edges to match or paint them with gold paint, then seal the frame with matt or satin oil-based varnish to prevent any further tarnishing.

Batons were fixed to the back of our frame to hold the picture with pins; MDF is quite heavy, so it needs a strong fixing to take the weight when it is hung on a wall. This frame would look just as wonderful with a mirror in it.

7 Mix matt or satin water-based varnish with acrylic tube paints, here Monestial Blue and Hooker's Green were used, diluting the paint first with a little water; using a small brush, paint this over the flat background, accentuating the raised design.

8 When the glaze is dry, antique the raised mouldings by coating all of a small section at a time with brown emulsion, ensuring it goes into all indentations; wipe off the emulsion across all the high points immediately with kitchen paper, to reveal gold highlights.

LEFT. This desk was beautifully made, but of dull oak. To cheer it up, having first rubbed it down with medium sandpaper to give it a key, it was painted with blue-green matt emulsion. When dry, this was distressed by rubbing carefully with the grain, again with medium sandpaper. To age the colour, it was then given a streaky coat of shellac. The design was drawn on the desk with blackboard chalk, the spacing being checked with a ruler, and was then painted in acrylics. After this, the whole piece was antiqued with Raw Umber oil-tube paint, mixed with white spirit to the consistency of very thin cream; it was finally varnished with satin oil-based varnish.

The photograph frame was made in the same way, but without tarnishing. Instead, brown emulsion was painted all over the frame, a section at a time, then wiped off. The lampshade is made from plastic-backed card. The design was traced on and painted in watery Venetian Red acrylic paint. No sealing was needed.

LEFT. This sombre oak chair was rubbed with medium sandpaper and given one coat of blue-green emulsion, lighter than the desk, then distressed with sandpaper and given a streaky coat of shellac, both going with the grain of the wood. It was sealed with a coat of satin oil-based varnish, to ensure durability.

The MDF wastepaper bin was sealed inside and out with acrylic primer/undercoat, and lightly sanded with fine sandpaper, after which two coats of deep bright red emulsion were given to the outside. A template was used to draw the outer line of the frame design on each side of the bin. Measuring in from this, the second line was drawn. Both were painted with a short lining brush and acrylic tube paint. The outside was crackle varnished, and Burnt Umber oil-tube paint was rubbed in. When dry, this was sealed with satin oil-based varnish. The inside of the bin was then painted with the same colour as the chair and streaked with shellac before it, too, was varnished.

The DINING ROOM

For our dining room, I wanted to evoke the Victorian era; a time which in the imagination consisted of calling cards, strolls in the park and slightly risqué late night suppers after the theatre, conjuring dark colours and chairs that could accommodate a bustle! For this reason, the shape of the chairs is typical of that time, and to decorate them, bronze powder stencilling, which became popular in the first half of the nineteenth century, has been used. The technique is very different from modern stencilling, the design being made up by stencilling overlapping flowers, fruit and leaves individually, using gold bronze powder on a sticky surface. Over black, the shading of the powder gives a magical three-dimensional effect which is not achievable in any other way.

Tortoiseshell suggested itself as a match for the gold; the former was very popular during the Victorian era, although probably not in the way it has been used here! It also blended well with the carpet and exotic sideboard, which could have come from a Spanish galleon two or three centuries earlier. To balance the amount of black in the room, a matching colour was chosen for the glass-fronted cupboard, but in a much lighter tone, the golden theme being continued by picking out the mouldings with leaf.

A SIDEBOARD WITH PENWORK

Although modern, this beautifully-shaped sideboard was made out of old pine. I loved its cabriole legs and curly 'apron'. Because I wanted to decorate the piece with penwork, I had to stain the pine a deeper colour and make it as smooth as possible for the fine waterproof pens needed to draw the design. After staining with an oil-based wood stain, it was sealed with several coats of shellac, followed by several of white polish. Between each coat, the sideboard was sanded lightly, and it was rubbed with wire wool after the last coat. This process gradually helps to fill the grain and build up a smooth surface.

A design of this type must be carefully worked out on paper before it is traced on the wood. By drawing the piece to scale, it is possible to work out exactly how wide the borders should be, to choose the size of the central motifs, and to ensure that the design will fit at the corners. The border design used for the sideboard can be adjusted to fit a longer or shorter shape by simply lengthening or shortening the diagonal sweeps between curls. When you are happy with all the design elements, the motifs used for the centre or other areas can then be enlarged to the correct size on a photocopier.

The most convenient way to draw this particular central design was to make a cardboard template of the peaked shaping. You can use Blu-tak to hold this in position while you draw around it.

The scheme for the sideboard was identical at each end, and was adjusted to fit the front, drawers and top. The adjustments were worked out on the ink scale drawing, many combinations being first tried out in pencil, rubbed out and re-drawn, until I was happy with the effect. Because of their shape, the apron at the bottom of the front, and the tops of the legs needed special treatment. Again the plan was first worked out on paper, and I then used blackboard chalk to draw on the sideboard itself, until the right combination appeared.

To make the curls at the leg tops follow the cabriole shape, some of the design had to be applied freehand, with the existing border adapted by dividing it into segments. Having measured in from the edge and made a line of pencil dots, to show where the paler wood edging was to go, I drew one leg top, continuing the design to a point under the centre of the nearest drawer. After going over this with a pen, it was possible to take a tracing and reverse it for the other side; the middle area could then be filled with an appropriate section of the new tracing.

When the background has been filled in and all is dry, a design of this type should have a sealing coat of water-based varnish, followed by several coats of white polish. By rubbing with fine wire wool between coats, it is possible to achieve a glass-like finish. To make this water- and heat-resistant (which is not so necessary for smaller items, such as lamps or boxes) the final varnishing should be with oil-based varnish, which can be either satin or gloss – three to four coats if possible.

MATERIALS
Paints etc: wood stain (optional), shellac, white polish, medium and fine black waterproof pens, black acrylic craft paint, and water-based varnish.

Brushes: watercolour brushes, and 5–7.5cm (2–3in) varnish brush.

1 Prepare the surface, making it as smooth as possible, and divide it in four with chalk lines. With a ruler and pencil, draw the outer edge of the border (as a guideline), and use pale blue carbon paper to trace the border design on the wood.

2 Draw all border lines with a medium-thickness black waterproof pen and a ruler. Use a template to mark the shaping of the centre motif, measuring from the centre along the chalk lines to give a balanced shape and linking the shapes with curves.

3 After outlining the traced border with a fine waterproof black pen, an extra option is to draw a diamond shape in the centre of the motif with the medium pen, and also draw diagonals across the narrowest border to make it resemble inlay.

4 Using a small brush, carefully paint the background around the design with either black craft or acrylic tube paint. If using the latter, you may need two coats. When dry, seal with one coat of water-based varnish, as oil- or spirit-based varnish could cause the ink to run.

This adaptation of the trace-off design can be used as an alternative, depending on the needs of the item you are painting.

LEFT. The lamps were modern, and made of wood. First, they were sealed with acrylic primer/undercoat, and given a second coat of the same paint. For an ivory look, the surface was then streaked with shellac, going down the length of the column. Next, water-based size was accurately applied to the mouldings, which were then gilded with Dutch metal leaf (see page 33). The whole surface was then crackled (see page 34), and Raw Umber oil-tube paint was rubbed into the cracks.

For the parchment shades, a miniature version of the template used for the sideboard was made. Each shade was placed over a circle divided into thirty-two equal segments, and the divisions were marked on the bottom of the shade with a pencil. The template shape was drawn at each mark, and the shapes were joined with curved lines. For the top edge, the same guide was used, but this time only alternate segments were marked. The shapes were painted with black acrylic tube paint; there was no need to seal the design.

LEFT. The modern mahogany chairs were first sealed with shellac, which was sanded smooth when dry. Each chair was given a coat of black oil-based eggshell paint, lightly sanded, and then given a second coat (emulsion could have been used instead).

The design for the back was planned by drawing through the stencils on paper. The chair was laid on its back and the top bar was given a sparing coat of oil-based varnish. After about twenty minutes, bronze powder was applied through the stencil, working from the central flower outward (see page 41). The lower bar was decorated in the same way.

Water-based size was applied accurately to the seat mouldings, leg tops and detail on the back (the oil-based paint was first wiped with rottenstone on a damp sponge to enable the size to adhere). Gold powder was dabbed on sparingly with a fitch and was left to dry overnight, then gently misted with oil-based spray varnish. The whole chair was finished with a coat of satin oil-based varnish.

LEFT. *Surprisingly, this table was white formica with an enamel base; both were keyed with medium wet-and-dry paper, then given two coats of black oil-based eggshell paint, and lightly sanded when dry. Using a protractor, the circular top was divided into ten 36° sections. Each of these was divided in half again for the points of the star. Having decided how long the points should be, they were measured out and the angles joined with a ruler and pencil. Leaving a black central circle, two base coats of yellow eggshell were given to the star, then every other panel was masked with tape and tortoiseshelled (see page 30). After drying for two or three days, the whole star was coated with water-based varnish and the remaining panels tortoiseshelled.*

A piece of card was cut and notched as a guide to mark the desired distance of the gold line from the table edge. Pencil dots were made every inch or so around the edge of the table, then joined. Using a short lining brush, the line

was painted with water-based goldsize. Narrow overlapping strips of transfer Dutch metal leaf were applied to the sized line. When dry, the loose bits were removed (see page 33), and the table sealed with three coats of oil-based varnish.

The table mats were done in the same way as the star, but with the black centre added afterwards.

LEFT. *The little cupboard – a bargain buy – was covered with ancient white gloss, so it was keyed with medium sandpaper; chips were patched with white acrylic primer/undercoat, after which came a complete coat of the same, followed when dry by a coat of pale corn-coloured emulsion. The mouldings were picked out in Dutch metal leaf; the whole was crackle varnished, and Raw Umber was rubbed into the cracks. Two coats of satin oil-based varnish finished the outside. The inside, which was shabby, was painted with black emulsion and the shelves covered in black sticky-backed felt.*

The
BREAKFAST
ROOM

With the rush of getting everyone off to work in the morning, as well as making sure children have eaten something and remembered their homework, it's a luxury to have a cheerful room, set apart from the kitchen, in which to organize at least a few minutes tranquility before the onslaught of the day. Here, breakfast can be laid the night before, avoiding chaos in the morning.

For the design on the cupboard doors, I wanted to imitate the Pennsylvanian Dutch style, brought to America by the early settlers from Bavaria. The colours were taken from books on Austro/German painted furniture, acquired while on a joyous visit to a museum in Munich. Instead of attempting to paint completely freehand this time, I have utilized a stencil, included in the kit at the back of the book, to block the shapes in with white paint, then painted watery shaded washes over the base so that it still looks as if it has been painted freehand. This technique is much easier than freehand painting, however, and the finished result is more soft and transparent than the original inspiration which, repeated on so many doors, might have been overpowering.

The pale antiqued turquoise that has been used for the background colour is typical of Bavarian furniture, and the finished effect gives us a welcoming cheerful room – a perfect place in which to start the day.

STENCILLED CUPBOARD DOORS

MATERIALS
Paints etc: Unibond glue, emulsion (greeny blue matt and cream), white acrylic primer/under-coat, meths, oil-based metal primer, water-colours (Prussian Blue, Yellow Ochre, Light Red and crimson), acrylic tubes (Payne's Grey, Venetian Red and white), oil tubes (Raw Umber, white and Payne's Grey), methylated spirit, white spirit, and oil-based varnish.

Brushes: 5cm (2in) decorator's, 12mm (½in) fitch, small and medium watercolour, short lining, and varnish brushes.

This breakfast room was decidedly sorry for itself! How many of us have wondered if we could do something drastic to cheer up old Formica units rather than face the huge expense and inconvenience of having new units fitted? It is possible, and in lots of different ways, with or without a design, the most important factor being to ensure that the new paint adheres. These doors were cleaned, then keyed with wet-and-dry paper, followed by a coat of Unibond glue, diluted with a little water.

Having drawn the units on paper and planned the size of the panels, a template was made for the panel outline. The simplest way to ensure that the top shaping of a design of this type is even is to fold a sheet of paper vertically in half, and draw one side of the panel shape; cut along the marked line, and then unfold the paper to give you the complete shape. The paper can then be glued to cardboard and cut out, to make a template. When using the template to mark out panels, it helps if you divide each door with horizontal and vertical chalk lines across the centre, using these to measure that the spacing is even on each side, and that all door panels in a row are level.

When painting the panels with their cream emulsion base, it doesn't matter if the undercoat shows through a little. Watercolours from an artist's paintbox were used over the white stencilling. First, the leaves were painted with watery Prussian Blue, a small, unpainted white highlight being left on the top left side of each (*see page 44*). A Yellow Ochre wash was added to the light side of the leaves; this blends with the blue, tinting it green in the middle.

For the rose, a mixture of Crimson and Light Red was painted round the side of the ball shape furthest from the light (*see page 46*). This was blended with clean water towards the lightest part, each petal being treated in the same way. While the paint is still wet or when dry, a deeper coral can be used to emphasize the shady side, and finally a touch of Prussian Blue can be added for the darkest shadows.

The berries were painted with Light Red in the same way, the shadows for both these and the tulips being deepened with Prussian Blue. Prussian Blue alone was used for the daisy-shaped flowers. These, and all the leaves, were finally shaded on the sides away from the light with a stronger mixture of this.

Venetian Red, mixed with white acrylic tube paint, was used for the outline. The antiquing glaze (*see step 8*) was painted all over, allowed to dry for a few minutes, then partly removed and blended with paper towel. An oil-based metal primer was used for the handles. When dry, after a day or two, at least two coats of oil-based varnish should be applied to make the surface washable.

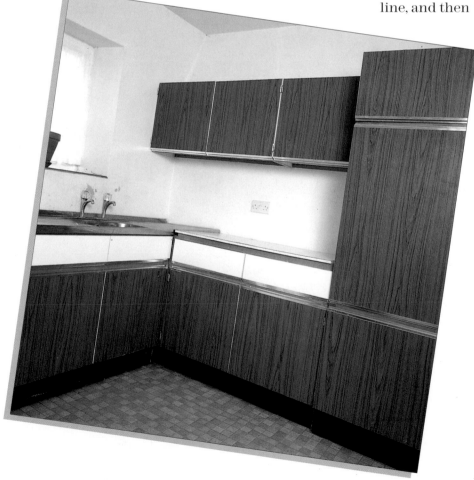

1 Clean well with sugar soap or detergent to remove any grease, then rub the surface and handles thoroughly with medium wet-and-dry paper to make a key. Dilute Unibond glue with 1-2 parts of water, depending on its thickness, and paint it over the doors.

2 When dry, apply three coats of greeny blue emulsion, drying between coats; lay the paint on in all directions, then while each coat is still wet draw the brush from top to bottom of the door, so the brushmarks are parallel (the final coat can be thicker so the marks show).

3 Mix Payne's Grey acrylic tube paint with water to the consistency of coffee, and paint it sparingly over the surface, going from top to bottom. When dry, rub the surplus off the tops of the brushmarks, using methylated spirit on paper towel (see page 20).

4 Make a template for the panel out of card; divide the door in four with blackboard chalk and a ruler. Draw round the template, then paint the panel in a cream emulsion, using a smaller brush, such as a fitch, and again with brushmarks going up and down.

This adaptation of the stencil can be used as an alternative trace-off design, depending on the needs of the item you are painting.

5 Divide the panel into six with chalk. Stencil the central rose first, working outwards from this. Dip a stencil brush into white acrylic primer/undercoat, dabbing any surplus off on paper towel before using the brush. Join stalks and leaves with a small brush.

6 First paint all the leaves and branches with washy Prussian Blue watercolour, leaving a small white highlight unpainted on the sides nearest to the light; here, to the left and above, add a wash of Yellow Ochre only to that side, giving the blue a greenish tinge.

RIGHT. The finished room looks decidedly more welcoming! By using watercolour over the white stencils, a very soft effect has been achieved. When the antiquing was dry, the handles were painted with a grey-blue metal paint and allowed to dry over-night before they and the doors were given two coats of satin oil-based varnish. For even greater durability, the doors could have been given a first coat of tough yacht varnish, lightly sanded when dry with fine sandpaper, and finished with a coat of satin varnish. Remember that oil-based varnish may feel dry the next day, but for maximum hardness, it will take about two weeks to cure.

A coral acrylic scumble glaze was mixed for the walls, to complement the stencil colours; this was painted on a cream silk vinyl background in sections and ragged (see page 27).

7 The tulips are striped from the petal tips downwards, and up from the base with Yellow Ochre and Light Red, leaving some white showing. Emphasize all the shadows with Prussian Blue, even adding it to the reds and pinks for their darkest tones.

8 With a small lining brush and using acrylic tube paint, paint a line round the panel, then antique it with a glaze of three parts Raw Umber, one part Payne's Grey and one and a half parts white oil tube paint, mixed with white spirit to a tea consistency.

LEFT. The table and chairs were treated in a similar way to the cupboard panels. The varnished pine table needed keying with medium sandpaper; the chairs were stripped, so no sanding was needed, but a coat of sanding sealer was given before painting. All were painted with cream emulsion, the brushstrokes going with the grain of the wood. Some emulsion was distressed off with medium sandpaper, revealing the wood.

The table design was planned on paper, using the same stencils as for the doors. For the border, a template was used with acrylic paint, the shape being shaded and highlighted to give a three-dimensional impression. The template was reduced in size for the chair backs and legs.

ABOVE. The modern enamel breadbin was rubbed down with sandpaper, sprayed with metal primer, then given a coat of cream emulsion, the brushmarks running down or round, as appropriate. The design, which was inspired by a Spanish flowerpot, was painted in acrylic tube paint, and finished with water- and then oil-based varnish.

The MDF kitchen top was sealed with acrylic primer/undercoat, followed after lightly sanding by two coats of pale grey emulsion and a coat of satin water-based varnish. Acrylic scumble glaze was tinted a deeper grey with black and white gouache, applied in diagonal patches and 'frottaged' (see page 27). The result, after several coats of satin oil-based varnish, looks rather like slate and blends well with the cupboards.

The
KITCHEN

Since our kitchen had to be fitted into quite a small area, a galley design was the only arrangement that would offer sufficient worktop space. Planning this kitchen, which is on the top floor of my school, took a great deal of measuring, drawing to scale, thinking and re-thinking, but after much dovetailing, I now have a very convenient, workable kitchen, in spite of its small size, though the lack of cupboard space necessitated a pole to hang saucepans on.

One of my problems was the high, barn-like ceiling, with its dark beams, which can have a chilling effect in winter, to counteract this, the kitchen needed to have a countrified look and a warm, welcoming colour scheme. Terracotta was the answer to both these demands, but a complete covering of terracotta would have been a little overpowering; by using it only for the panels, while keeping the background neutral, the impact of the colour was softened, and the pleasing shapes of the panels themselves are emphasized.

To avoid harsh solidity, both the frames and the panels have been distressed, the former by rubbing back to the wood in places, and the latter by using a random texture under the terracotta, giving a very soft effect. Fridge freezers, if not enclosed, can spoil the look of a kitchen, so it was a delightful challenge to paint this one to match the units.

A RUSTIC CHAIR

MATERIALS
Paints etc: terracotta emulsion, acrylic tube paints (white, Burnt Umber and Venetian Red), brown stain wax, and water-based varnish.

Brushes: small watercolour, short lining, fitch, and 2.5cm (1in) varnish or decorator's brushes.

This modern pine chair needed to match the kitchen units, which are cream, terracotta and green, but the colours were deliberately kept to a minimum so that the chairs will fit into almost any colour scheme. Instead of choosing cream for the base coat and using the other colours for the design, I decided that it would look prettier if this were reversed, with the darker terracotta for the background, and a pale design.

The chair had a finish of light varnish, so it had to be keyed first by rubbing with medium sandpaper. The following coat of terracotta emulsion was put on fairly sparingly, in the direction of the grain, allowing the wood colour to shine through a little. In order to keep the rustic feeling that had been selected for the kitchen, the heart is in the Pennsylvanian Dutch style, but the curving branches fascinated me twenty years ago when I saw them on a painted ceiling in the Uffizi Gallery in Florence.

Once you have traced the design on a chair you can use the outline as a guide, but add leaves with a certain degree of freedom to a whole set of chairs. The aim is that they should match each other but still have the individuality of freehand painting. A photocopier can be used to enlarge or reduce the design to fit on any size of facet.

When cutting out the tracing, it should be left about 12mm (½in) larger all around than the facet on which it is to be traced. The carbon paper should be slightly smaller, so that it can be taped to the back of the design or just slid under it. Use a pencil or biro to trace the outline, tracing firmly. Enlarge the main design by 250 per cent for the chair seat, and prune away the outermost branches.

When the design for the chair is finished, it can be given a coat of brown stain wax, to antique it. Some waxes can dissolve acrylics, so before doing this, paint some of the emulsion and acrylic tube paint used for the design on a piece of card, and test the wax over it. To avoid any problems, give the design a coat of matt or satin acrylic varnish first, to protect it (the wax will adhere best to a matt finish).

An alternative way to paint the design would be to use two colours on the brush for each leaf. For example, mix two thick creamy puddles of acrylic paint on a plate; say, Raw Umber and turquoise, or Yellow Ochre and Monestial Blue. Lay one side of the brush in the first colour; turn it over and lay the other side in the second. Press the brush down where the two colours meet to create beautifully variegated leaves, which can be left as they are or shaded, as for our chair.

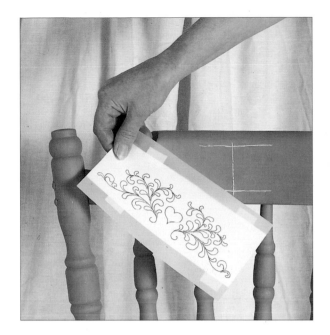

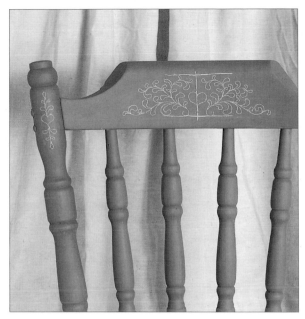

1 Key with sandpaper, then paint one coat of terracotta emulsion, brushing in the direction of the wood grain. Measure and mark the centre of the chair back panel with chalk. Cut the tracing to fit, attaching carbon paper to the underside with masking tape.

2 Lay the chair on its back, and place the heart on the central line, so the branches are level at each side. Working from the centre outwards, trace the heart and branches, then the leaves. Use smaller designs on uprights, and an enlarged photocopy on the seat.

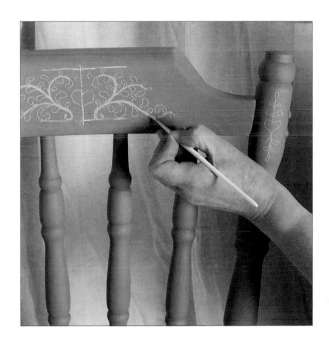

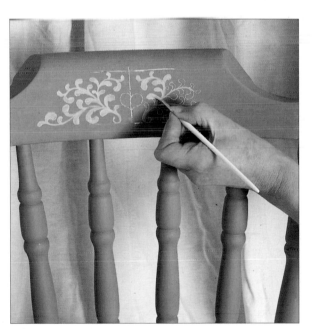

3 Using a small watercolour brush, paint the branches with white acrylic tube paint and water, tinted with a little Burnt Umber, mixed on a plate to a creamy consistency so that the paint glides easily over the emulsion, making the curves as smooth as possible.

4 For the leaves, load the whole length of the brush with the same creamy mixture and, starting at each rounded tip, press the bristles down firmly, lifting and curving them towards the branch, taking the brush off with a neat slant at the join.

This adaptation of the trace-off design can be used as an alternative, depending on the needs of the item you are painting.

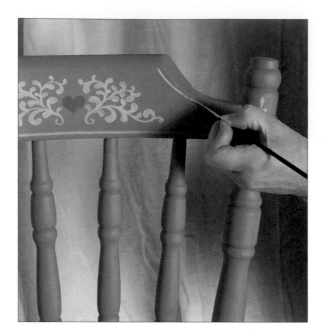

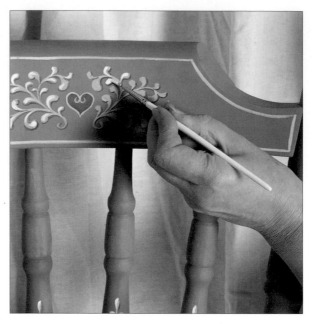

5 Paint the heart with Venetian Red, wiping off all chalk marks when dry. Next, using a short lining brush and the same mixture as for the leaves, paint a line round the panel 6mm (¼in) in from the edge either painting freehand (see page 42) or using a pencil line.

6 Outline the heart with off-white, then mix Burnt Umber with a little white for the shadows, painting these under and to the right of each element, as if the design were a carving and the light were coming from the top left-hand corner.

RIGHT. When the wax has dried, use a soft cloth and lots of elbow grease to polish to a beautiful deep shine, creating the patina of years of use. The thickly painted highlights will catch the tinted wax, making their textured brushmarks look oil-painted.

For extra durability, the chairs could have been varnished with a matt varnish before waxing, but wax itself forms a waterproof film nearly as protective as varnish, and subsequent layers of tinted or plain wax will increase the protection.

The design could be adapted to a more upright panel by turning the bottoms of the two wings of branches to face each other, with or without the heart between them. The design on the uprights could also be used as a border.

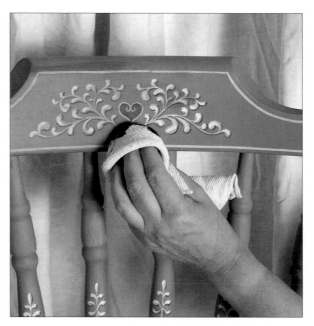

7 Using a thicker mixture of white acrylic, paint a small highlight on the curve of each leaf, facing the top lefthand corner, where the imaginary light is coming from; here, if the paint is used more thickly, the brushmarks will enhance the subsequent antiquing.

8 When all is dry, apply brown stain wax, streaking it on with a cloth and using a fitch to paint it into the turnings of the back and legs. Blend the edges with a cloth. Test the wax over a small area of the paint first, to check that the wax will not dissolve it.

LEFT. *The kitchen units were modern lacquered oak, whereas the fridge-freezer was white enamel. First, they were all keyed with wet-and-dry paper. The fridge-freezer was coated with Unibond glue diluted with water, to ensure that the paint would adhere, then silk vinyl water-based paint in a similar colour to the oak of the cupboards. Next, all surfaces were painted in acrylic primer/ undercoat. For the panel centres, the same paint was thickened with powdered Polyfilla and brushed randomly in all directions. When dry, this was coated with cream emulsion and left to dry. Red oxide emulsion was diluted with four parts of water and painted sparingly over the ceam. When dry, it was partially rubbed off with meths (see page 20), emphasizing the original brushmarks. The outer borders of the units were distressed with sandpaper to reveal the wood. All panels were given a washy green border of acrylic paint mixed with acrylic varnish.*

LEFT. *The rocking chair started life as an ordinary chair, bought at auction. The shape demanded rockers, so a kindly joiner obliged. The chair was painted, so it had to be keyed with sandpaper, followed by acrylic primer/undercoat, a coat of turquoise emulsion, and then one of satin acrylic varnish. A dark green glaze made with artists' acrylic medium mixed with Hooker's Green acrylic tube paint was dragged over the blue, following the grain of the wood. Having picked out some turnings in off-white, the design was hand-painted in Cadmium Red, Hooker's Green, turquoise and white acrylic tube paints. It was finished with the brown stain wax used for the terracotta chairs.*

The
CONSERVATORY

*D*oesn't this conservatory remind you of a sunny summer's day? The sort we remember having as children, when every summer was wonderful! Because there is so much glass, it is beautifully light, and ideal for reading, painting or stitchery, all of which can be difficult by electric light. So to make this room comfortable, but practical as well, and able to cope with the necessary watering, the chairs that have been used can withstand the odd splash, and are also very easy to carry into the garden when needed. The table is both elegant and sensible; perfect for lunching at or re-potting on.

The designs for the cushions were adapted from the stencil for the chair; the inspiration came from the feeling that this conservatory belongs to the late nineteenth century. I visualize tiny waists, large hats and upright men with stiff collars and beards. The association of ideas led me to the Arts and Crafts movement and the pottery of William de Morgan, with its beautifully simplified, stylized flowers and leaves; thus we have leaves which blend with the real foliage, the shade of green being altered to that of verdigris, mixed with cream and a touch of terracotta, one of its complementary shades.

A LEAFY DIRECTOR'S CHAIR

MATERIALS
Paints etc: white acrylic primer/undercoat, jade emulsion, silk paints (emerald, black and turquoise), and water-based varnish.

Brushes: stencil, watercolour, and 2.5cm (1in) varnish or decorator's brushes.

Director's chairs can be bought in all sorts of colours. Fitting in with any scheme or style, they are very comfortable and amazingly inexpensive, and you can fold them neatly away if and when necessary. Here, cream chairs have been chosen to blend with our conservatory, but fabric of any colour, even black, could be used with these white stencils. The stencils used in the breakfast room or the dining room could equally well be used here.

I love greeny blues and verdigris, and the colours picked for these chairs were destined to be no exception! Once the canvas had been removed, the frames, being new, needed a little

sanding to remove the varnish before they were painted with one coat of jade emulsion. This was then distressed with sandpaper to reveal some of the wood beneath, especially on the edges.

The canvas was laid on a flat surface and the chalk guidelines drawn without any further preparation. To prevent paint soaking through to the underlying surface, especially when using thinner fabrics such as the cushion material, you may wish to put several layers of old newspaper underneath the fabric. When stencilling, use the paint quite thickly so that the weave of the fabric is thoroughly covered.

When the emulsion has dried, mix silk paints on a plate with water. The outline must be painted just inside the edge of the white stencil to prevent the silk paint bleeding into the unpainted canvas. When painting the strap-shaped leaves, imagine that the light is coming from the top lefthand corner; paint the darker green line to the right and below each one, blending across it with clean water, and still leaving a dry white border the other side.

While still wet, the colours can be strengthened by adding to them, or reduced by blotting with paper towel, revealing the white like a highlight. Repeat the same process for all the leaves, painting in the branch very carefully with a small brush.

When dry, iron the wrong side of the canvas with a hot iron, following the manufacturer's instuctions. Silk dyed fabrics are generally washable if the instructions are followed correctly, but the undercoat is obviously likely to suffer if the fabric is washed in the normal way and may affect the dyes themselves. It would therefore be wise to spray the finished chair or cushion covers with a dust repellant, for added protection. (For completely washable covers, omit the paint and use white fabric and silk paints alone.) The chair frame was finished with two coats of satin water-based varnish.

1 Chalk centred guidelines dividing the canvas in four. Using white acrylic primer/undercoat, stencil the large centre leaf on half of it, horizontally, then stencil the smaller leaves and branches, repeating the mirror image on the other half.

2 When the white paint is dry, use silk paints to mix a dark green on a plate from emerald and a little black. Dilute the paint with some water and paint a line a little in from the edge of a leaf, to prevent paint bleeding onto the unsealed canvas.

3 While the paint is still wet, rinse the brush, dip it in clean water and run it down the inside of the line to dilute and blend the paint, spreading it across the leaf, but leaving the other edge white. Encircle larger leaves with dark green, blending it towards the centre.

4 Leave a small margin of dry white to prevent the colours bleeding onto the canvas. Add turquoise to the pale wet edge of the strap-shaped leaves, still leaving a small margin of dry white paint of the further side, and to the centre of the larger leaves in a V shape.

This adaptation of the stencil can be used as an alternative trace-off design, depending on the needs of the item you are painting.

95

LEFT. When the silk paint is thoroughly dry, press the wrong side of the fabric with a hot iron to fix the colour, following the manufacturer's instructions. The chair frames were given two coats of satin water-based varnish. The finished chairs invite relaxation on a sunny day, and would look equally appealing in any room, painted to match an existing colour scheme.

The cages are made of bamboo, which needed no preparation. For a verdigris finish, white liming paste was used, tinted to the correct colour with Veridian gouache tube paint mixed with a little black. The liming paste was painted all over the bars and into all nooks and crannies with a fitch. A damp cloth was used to wipe a little dried (but water-soluble) paste from the highlights, to reveal the golden bamboo. For the larger cage, a little gold wax was applied here and there to emphasize the metallic look. Should you wish to varnish, use a matt oil-based type, so as not to disturb the paste.

LEFT. Our table top was made out of MDF to fit metal legs found in a junk shop. After the sealing coat of acrylic primer/undercoat had dried, ready-mixed fine-surface filler was applied with a paint brush.

First, random patches were painted on the surface and patted with a wire brush to give them peaks, then swirls of filler were applied between and overlapping the original patches, rather like a fast running river, until the whole table top was covered. When dry, it was rubbed with medium sandpaper to make it smoother, then given a sparing coat of pale jade emulsion, which skimmed the peaks, leaving most of the indentations white.

When this had dried, a glaze of Raw Umber oil-tube paint and white spirit, the consistency of milk, was painted over generously, into all the indentations, and the surplus wiped off with paper towel.

The next day the table was finished with two coats of satin oil-based varnish.

RIGHT. For both these garden cushions the same method has been used as for the chairs, but the calico chosen was thinner than the chair canvas, enabling the fabric to be sewn afterwards. Some gold silk paint was added after the design was dry, using brushstrokes as on page 45. Before sewing the covers, the paint was fixed by pressing with a hot iron on the wrong side.

The cane chair was treated with liming paste in the same way as the cages. This time the paste was tinted with Raw Umber and Raw Sienna gouache to match the canvas of the chairs. Powder pigments or universal stainers could equally well be used. The paste was painted all over the chair and allowed to dry, then partially wiped off with a damp cloth. The chair was sealed with matt oil-based varnish.

RIGHT. The terracotta pot on the right was sealed inside and out with satin water-based varnish and painted sparingly with liming paste, the majority wiped off when dry with a damp cloth. The border was traced, and painted in Venetian Red acrylic tube paint, followed by water-based goldsize, with gold bronze powder thinly patted on from a brush. This was shaded with Burnt Umber acrylic tube paint and sealed with oil-based varnish. The plaster pedestal was painted with water then, while wet, shellac. When dry, liming wax was painted all over with a fitch, then taken from highlights with paper towel.

The plastic urn (left) was sealed with Unibond glue and water. Random patches were gilded with silver leaf. Gum arabic was applied to all but the leaf, then white acrylic primer/undercoat, overlapping the leaf slightly. When dry, the cracked paint was antiqued with a creamy mixture of Raw Umber oil tube paint and white spirit, sealed when dry with two coats of oil-based varnish.

The
BEDROOM

Because of its beams, this bedroom has a rustic feel; it would be very easy to make the painted furniture too new or grand looking. Simplicity and understatement were called for, therefore the colours needed to be subdued and restricted to the minimum. They also needed to match the existing carpets and curtains, yet still blend in with any other colour scheme, should the decor be changed at a later date.

Distressing the cupboard doors and chest helped them to blend into the atmosphere of the room better than if the paint were solid, and the distressed finish also reduced the sheer size of the doors by breaking up the surface. All the pieces were antiqued to make the white background less stark. Pale shades of grey blue were chosen for the designs, to contrast with the gold of the revealed pine yet tone with the carpet. Blues can be quite cold if used on their own, so touches of my beloved coral have been added in the shape of the cushion and lampshade, which pick out the colour of the lilies in the painting, as does its inner mount. This addition not only warms up the whole room, making it more welcoming, but being a complementary colour, the coral intensifies the blue, making it less grey-looking. (Try covering up the top half of the picture on page 105, and you'll see what I mean!)

GARLANDED DOORS

MATERIALS
Paints etc: white spirit, acrylic primer/undercoat, pale blue emulsion, acrylic tube paints (Hooker's Green, Ultramarine, Payne's Grey and white), and oil tube paints (Raw Umber and Raw Sienna), and satin water-based varnish.

Brushes: large and medium watercolour, and 2.5–5cm (1–2in) varnish or decorator's brushes.

Whatever their style, built-in wardrobe doors always cover a large area. They can be painted to match the walls, making them as invisible as possible, or they can be turned into a feature. These doors, made from tongued-and-grooved pine, took up a whole wall of the room, and the surface offered more of a challenge than flat doors. The chosen design could, however, be used just as easily on any style of door.

The doors were first removed and the round handles taken off. The wood had been waxed, so this finish had to be removed by rubbing with white spirit and wire wool (*see page 15*) in order to make the paint stick. The doors were then coated with acrylic primer/undercoat, the brushmarks going with the grain of the wood, but any emulsion could have been used. When distressing a previously-

waxed surface, care needs to be taken in case there is some remaining wax, which could cause more paint to come off than you would want!

Having drawn the doors on paper and planned the design, part of the leaf swag was stencilled at the top of each door, on each side, with pale blue emulsion. Measure carefully, leaving enough room for the flower swag tracing to overlap the leaf swags by a fraction. The straight leaf stencil was then used down the sides, with a longer drop for the outer doors, gradually getting shorter towards the centre.

Next, the flower swags and bunches for the middle doors were traced on and painted with the same blue emulsion mixed with a little water; a small amount of Hooker's Green acrylic tube paint was added for the leaves and the bows. The flowers and leaves were then shaded and highlighted as described in steps 3 and 4, the aim being to create shadows that would give the effect of a carved design. The leaf swags and drops were also shaded, but as they are quite small, no highlight was necessary.

The depths of the shadows were then emphasized with a darker tone, and the lightest part of the highlights stroked with white. Half the leaves, lengthways, were also shaded, using a little more green than for the flowers.

When all was done, the doors were toned down by antiquing them with half-and-half Raw Umber and Raw Sienna oil tube paint, mixed with white spirit to the consistency of tea. This was painted all over, then after a few minutes some was wiped off in streaks, and the remaining streaks were blended at the edges with paper towel.

The next day, when the glaze was dry, it was varnished with two coats of satin water-based varnish (you could use an oil-based varnish if you prefer).

The metal hinges were left black, but they could have been painted with metal primer, followed by an oil-based paint.

1 De-wax, then paint the doors with one coat of acrylic primer/undercoat, going with the grain. Distress with sandpaper when dry. Measure and mark the stencil positions with pencil, then attach them with Blu-tak and stencil with blue emulsion.

2 Having left room in the middle for the rosy tracing, this and the bows can now be positioned with Blu-tak; slip carbon behind them and trace both with a biro or pencil, then paint with blue emulsion plus a little water. For the bows, add a little Hooker's Green to the blue.

3 Use the same blue-green mixture for the leaves, then Payne's Grey and Ultramarine are added to this colour to mix a deeper shade for the shadows, which fall to the right of and below each element, since the window is to the left.

4 For the highlights at the top and left of each flower, a little shadow colour is mixed into white, and applied round the 'ball' and the opposite petals. The deepest part of the shadows are then darkened and the lightest part of the highlights touched with white.

This adaptation of the design can be used as an alternative trace-off design, depending on the needs of the item you are painting.

LEFT. *From this distance one can see how the design has helped to reduce the size of the doors by drawing the eye to the central two, with their bunches of flowers, the tracing being reversed for the second so that the bunches mirror-image each other. The same applies to the swags and bows above, where the tracing was reversed for doors two and four.*

The drops at each end of the swags increase in length as they get further from the centre, helping to frame the doors and again visually reducing their overall size.

RIGHT. *The chest of drawers, which was of old waxed pine, was prepared in the same way as the wardrobe. The chest decoration was designed to scale on paper, then drawn on the chest with a ruler and chalk. First, the outer lines were painted with a thick lining brush and a mixture of acrylic tube paint in the same colours as the wardrobe, plus white. Then a finer lining brush was used for the geometric lines on the front, sides and top. Using the same colour and*

working freehand, leaves were painted on half the lines (the drop stencil could be used instead).

All was shaded like the wardrobe, and the panels were added. The design was lightly distressed with fine sandpaper, then antiqued, one facet at a time, and varnished in the same way as for the doors.

Made from new pine, the picture frame was stained with acrylic tube paint diluted with water to a runny consistency, painted on, and allowed to soak in. For the outer frame, Ultramarine was used, while a mixture of Cadmium Red and Yellow Ochre (making coral) stained the inner fillet. When these had dried, they were sealed with sanding sealer. When dry, the outer frame was stroked with a wire brush in the direction of the grain to open it up; liming wax tinted with Ultramarine oil-tube paint was rubbed on, wiped off the raised parts of the moulding, then polished with a soft cloth when dry.

The lamp was treated in the same way as those in the dining room (see page 72).

RIGHT. *Ignoring all chips, the old green paint of the chair was keyed with an allover rub. It was given two coats of acrylic primer/undercoat, and a sparing coat of pale blue. This was rubbed with fine sandpaper to reveal some of the white. The panel was drawn with pencil and painted with off-white emulsion. The lines were painted in acrylic with a short lining brush. The panel was filled with roses and buds (see page 46), with leaves arranged to balance and fill the space. The chair was antiqued and then finished with two coats of matt oil-based varnish.*

The MDF bin was given two coats of acrylic primer on the outside and blue emulsion inside. Both were then sparingly streaked with watery mixes of blue-green acrylics. The design was stencilled in white primer, then shaded, and two coats of satin water-based varnish were applied.

The papier-mâché hatbox was coated with grey blue emulsion; the design was painted freehand with watery acrylic tube paint, and two coats of satin water-based varnish, tinted with brown stainer, were applied.

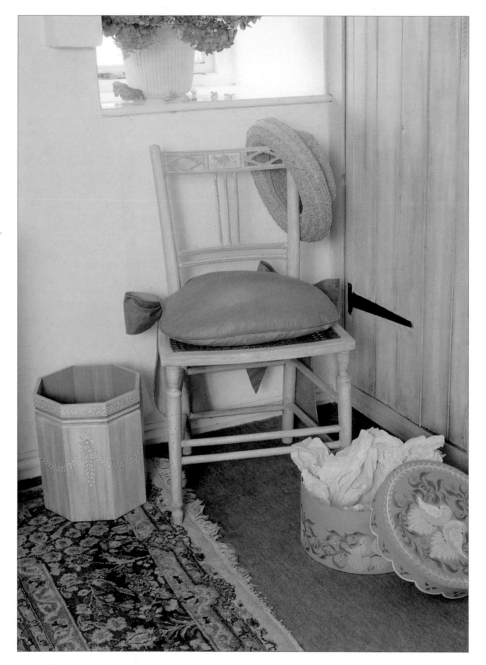

RIGHT. *This old bedhead was veneered. It was sanded, then sealed with acrylic primer, followed by the same paint mixed with powdered Polyfilla to give it texture (see page 31). The flowers and leaves, which were inspired by the fabric, were painted freehand in the same colours, a lining brush being used to emphasize the bevel. It was sealed with two coats of satin water-based varnish.*

The carved mirror frame was treated in the same way as the swag on page 103. The same acrylic colours were used as for the bedhead, except for the inner oval, which was painted red/brown, gilded with Dutch metal leaf, and distressed (see the frame on page 60).

The bedside tables, of modern plywood, were sealed with two coats of acrylic primer, then given random patches of gum arabic. When dry they were given a coat of green emulsion to match the lampshades. This cracked over the gum arabic and was further distressed by rubbing with medium sandpaper, to reveal the white undercoat on the edges and elsewhere. They were sealed with oil-based varnish.

The
BATHROOM

Having decided to try and transform an elderly, completely tiled bathroom with paint, rather than employing builders to demolish the tiles and re-plaster the walls, it was very difficult to settle on a design and choose the colours, the range of options being infinite.

Because bathrooms have water, dolphins came to mind. Beautiful, cheerful, smiling dolphins! But how to use them in a design? When in doubt, I turn to design reference books. To my delight I found that dolphins were one of the most popular components of Renaissance design, and frequently used in the fifteenth and sixteenth centuries. By the time this discovery had been made, my mind was teeming with the Renaissance and its swirling scrolls, so I determined to evolve a dolphin design inspired by that era.

Next, the colour – as I love the neutral greys and beiges of 'grisailles', those colours were a first choice, but they might have been a trifle dull on their own; something soft was needed, which would go with a warm beige without contrasting too much, so as a change from my usual corals, turquoises and emeralds, I chose pink, mixed with a touch of deeper burgundy to avoid it looking too sugary.

DOLPHIN TILES

MATERIALS
Paints etc: cream oil-based exterior undercoat, pink emulsion, water-based varnish, acrylic tube paints (crimson, Burnt Umber and white), and heavy-duty water-based floor varnish (or oil-based varnish).

Brushes: stencil, watercolour, and 5cm (2in) varnish or decorator's brushes.

For years, in different houses, I have lived with less than beautiful – dare I say ghastly – tiles, so I was determined to attempt to transform some one day. What could be a greater challenge than this bathroom, with its patterned tiles from floor to ceiling! When it was installed, the tiles were probably very fashionable and slightly daring, but a change was long overdue.

Not only were they patterned, but the pattern was indented, making it almost impossible to paint them with a small design, so a large single panel suggested itself. The design was worked out to scale on paper, and the tracings were then enlarged by a photocopier to the correct size for the wall panel, covering a number of A3 pieces of paper. A stencil was cut for the egg-and-dart border.

When the base coats were dry, the enlarged design sections were stuck to the wall with Blu-tak. I measured to find the centre, placing the shell first and working outwards from it. Once the edge of the design was established,

the best place for the border could be decided. This was then stencilled with ready-mixed pink emulsion, making sure that an 'egg' or 'dart' was at the centre, and working out to the corners. The paint was applied sparingly, leaving highlights on the eggs where the underlying cream could still be seen, and stopping short of the corners, which would be completed later.

Grey graphite carbon paper was used for the tracings in the bathroom. Remember that you can move the carbon as often as necessary without affecting the design, provided the tracings are attached to the wall. When all was traced, the design was removed and the outlines were filled in. A little water-based varnish was mixed with the emulsion to make it more soft and transparent. This was shaded and highlighted as described in steps 6–8.

The shadows and highlights were repeated on the stencilled border, then came the time to stand back and decide how best to deal with the corners. Here, a square with eight freehand petals was added, but a stencil or tracing could just as easily be used.

For the bath panel, the design was then printed to a smaller scale and re-arranged, with the dolphins swapped over and placed horizontally instead of upright. They were traced on and, after a careful check that the traced shapes were level, they were painted in the same way as the egg-and-dart border.

The surface here was prepared so that ordinary paints, including emulsion, could be used, but it is well worth experimenting with ceramic paints. These are specially designed to adhere to ceramic surfaces and include oil-based types, both opaque and transparent, and water-based paints. The latter can be used like watercolours, for a lovely range of soft, shaded effects, but the paints must be fixed by baking in an oven, following the manufacturer's instructions, so you can only use these paints on new tiles, before they are fixed to the wall.

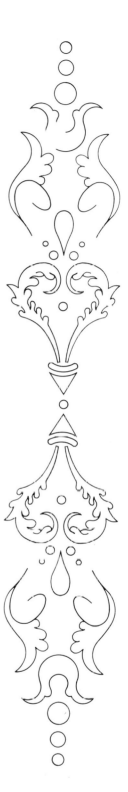

1 Having cleaned the old tiles well with sugar soap to remove all grease, mix Uni-bond glue to a paintable consistency with 1–2 parts of water and brush it on to key the surface. This should be allowed to dry at least overnight and will give the tiles a matt look.

2 Next, apply two coats of exterior oil-based undercoat in cream, allowing each a day to dry. An emulsion could be used instead, provided it is ultimately sealed with several coats of oil- or water-based varnish (make sure all the edges and grouting are cleaned).

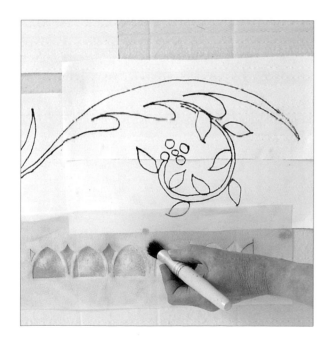

3 Enlarge the tracings on a photocopier to fit the area; tape the elements together, then measure and position them with Blu-tak or masking tape. Attach the border stencil and dab sparingly with pink emulsion, leaving some highlights on the eggs.

4 Slip some carbon paper between the tracings and the wall, taking a section at a time. Trace over the lines with a pencil or biro, moving the carbon when necessary. If the lines wobble a little on the uneven surface, they can be straightened when you are painting.

This adaptation of the trace-off design can be used as an alternative, depending on the needs of the item you are painting.

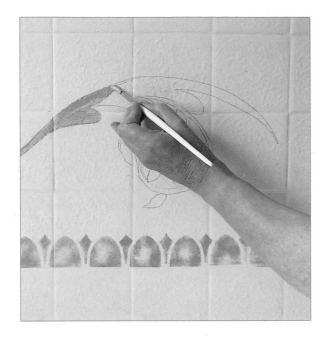

5 *Remove the tracings, then mix some of the emulsion used for the stencil with water-based varnish to make it more transparent and runny. Using a large watercolour brush, fill the traced outlines, keeping the brush-marks running in the direction of the contours.*

6 *Now put some of that mixture on a plate and add a little Crimson and Burnt Umber acrylic tube-paint, mixed with water. With the same brush, join the gaps in the stencilled border and paint shadows below and to the right of each element.*

RIGHT. The panels were given four coats of heavy-duty water-based floor varnish; each coat was allowed to dry thoroughly, and the tiles were lightly sanded before the final coat. All varnish needs time to cure, so don't clean for at least a week and then only gently.

The MDF screen was sealed with acrylic primer/undercoat, given two coats of cream emulsion, then a border painted with the pink emulsion and varnish mixture. The design was drawn on with chalk; painted freehand, using Burnt Umber and white acrylic tube paint, and shaded and highlighted like the tiles. A lining brush was used to outline the panels with a mixture of acrylic tube paints – Burnt Umber, Crimson and just a little white.

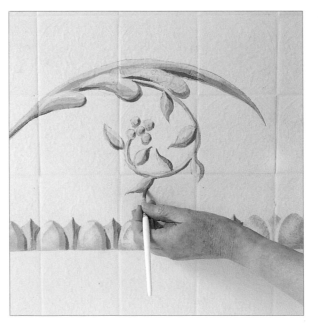

7 *For the highlights on the opposite side to the shadows, where the light would fall from the window on the left if the design was carved, mix a little white acrylic tube paint and water into the original mixture. Highlight the border in the same way.*

8 *Deepen the darkest shadows by adding a little more Crimson and Burnt Umber to the shadow mixture. Stand back to check the balance, adding stronger highlights and shadows as necessary. Seal with several coats of floor-quality acrylic varnish.*

LEFT. Loving its shape, I bought this little wash-stand years ago in a junk shop. Its bright green chipped gloss was well sanded down to key the surface, and it was then given two coats of acrylic primer/undercoat to mask the colour. Next came a coat of the cream emulsion used for the screen, followed by a coat of satin water-based varnish, to give it a sheen. One part of the pink emulsion was mixed with 2–3 parts of acrylic scumble glaze and dragged on with a small brush; a dry brush was also used, to re-define the drag where necessary, and the glaze was wiped off the edges and turnings of the legs. When the glaze was dry, the panels were lined, using a short lining brush and the same acrylic colours as for the lines on the screen. A circular template was cut from card and drawn round as a guide when painting the circle on the table top.

LEFT. This old oak frame was sanded and sealed with shellac to key it for the two coats of acrylic primer/undercoat to follow. The unpainted shells were then stuck to the frame with contact adhesive, applied to both surfaces. The frame was sprayed twice with white car primer, to give a pearly finish without disturbing the shells.

To tie in with the colour scheme, a narrow mount was cut and painted with a watery wash of crimson watercolour, starting at a corner and wetting the preceding 5cm (2in) or so, to prevent a hard line on the join. Some 5–7.5cm (2–3in) at a time were covered with the wash; this was allowed to sink in for a few seconds, then patted with paper towel to give a marbled effect. (For best results with this technique, occasionally go back, adding more of the wash and patting again.) There was no need to seal the frame and mount with varnish, as it was not likely to receive much wear and tear, but if you feel that your frame might suffer damage from damp, you could paint both with either an oil-based or spirit-based varnish.

A
CHILD'S
ROOM

At a price, it is possible to buy wonderful furniture for little people, but always remember they are not children for long. By the time they are teenagers, their taste will have changed drastically. The ideal solution is to paint inexpensive things for them, that can be re-painted at a later date.

Colour, rather than design, has been used to bind the projects for this room together. The brilliant green carpet was the starting point – what would go with it? In a nearby antique shop I found a little cup from the early 1800s. It had a bright yellow background, with a wreath of flowers in shades of orange, rust and purple, offset by leaves in the same green as the carpet. The kind shop owner allowed me to borrow it so I could match the colours.

The nearest background colour was Cadmium Yellow; the rust was Burnt Sienna. A blue was needed to make the green, so I tried several, mixing them with the yellow; the best match was achieved by using turquoise. To create the dull purple, a red was needed, and this proved to be Cadmium Red.

While mixing, I made a colour chart, trying each colour with another in varying amounts, then adding white and dabbing each of the many shades onto a piece of card. They harmonized perfectly with each other and with the carpet, so only those colours were used for all the projects.

TROMPE L'OEIL CHEST

MATERIALS
*Paints etc: acrylic
primer/undercoat, yellow
and turquoise emulsion,
acrylic tube paints
(Cadmium Red, Burnt
Sienna, Cadmium Yellow,
turquoise and white), and
water- or oil-based
varnish.*

*Brushes: watercolour
and 2.5–5cm (1–2in)
varnish or decorator's
brushes.*

Having often seen furniture with wonderful painted trompe l'oeil effects, the thought of a child's chest of drawers painted to look like shelves covered in favourite objects came irresistibly to mind.

The idea was planned on paper, initially by drawing the front of the chest to scale, then deciding where the 'eye level' point would be. By drawing lines fanning out from that point to the corners of the drawers, the perspective of the shelves and the toys and other objects on them could be established.

Children frequently sit and play on the floor, so the eye level point was chosen at the bottom of the central upright between the top drawers. From that point, pencil lines were ruled out to the drawer corners, then the perpendicular lines for the sides were ruled; horizontal lines, starting and ending where the perpendicular ones dissect the diagonals, gave us the ceilings and the backs of the shelves, then all that remained was the fun of putting things on them! All was

sketched on paper, including the round knobs,which would be painted separately and put on at the end.

The watery washes of acrylic tube paint that were used to block in the various colours on the chest were mixed on a plate and distributed evenly from shelf to shelf. The palette was restricted to mixtures of Cadmium Red, Cadmium Yellow, Burnt Sienna, turquoise and white.

When the back of the shelves around the toys and books was painted with turquoise emulsion, the chest immediately began to come to life! White acrylic primer/undercoat was added to the turquoise emulsion to make a lighter tone for the shelves and the right-hand wall. Since the imaginary light was coming from the left, that wall and the ceiling would be darker, so a little Burnt Sienna and turquoise acrylic tube paint was mixed into the emulsion for those sections.

When you paint each drawer, the primer and top coat should be taken around the sides up to the dovetail join or for the thickness of the drawer front, and also you should paint all inner edges of the main base for about 2.5cm (1in), so no bare wood will be visible if the drawers don't fit very well.

For the shadows which would turn the flat objects into three-dimensional ones, the same acrylic colours were used, each shade being darkened by mixing an opposite colour into it – the red or Burnt Sienna into the greens and turquoises, and visa versa. Since our imaginary light comes from the left, the shadows lie consistently to the right and below everything.

On the bottom two shelves, each object castes a deeper turquoise shadow to the right and/or below, its size being gauged from the depth and height of each item.

When all was finished, the body of the chest was given two coats of matching yellow emulsion, and both the chest and the knobs were varnished, the latter being attached to the chest when it was dry.

1 The chest, made from new wood, was sealed with acrylic primer/undercoat. Using a ruler and pencil, lines of perspective were drawn, as on the scale plan, fanning out from the centre to the corners, to mark out the positions of the shelves and shelf backs.

2 The components of the design on paper were individually traced and enlarged on a photocopier. They were cut out roughly, attached to the chest with Blu-tak and, using carbon paper, traced on – the undermost ones first, followed by the overlapping top layer.

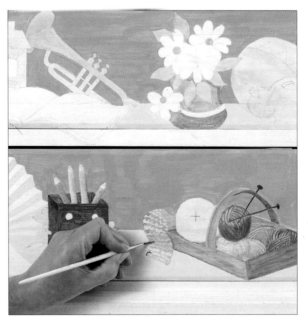

3 Having blocked in most of the contents with an evenly balanced group of watery acrylic washes, which were mixed from a restricted palette of four colours and white, the back wall was painted in round the toys and books with turquoise emulsion.

4 When the walls, floor and ceiling were painted, all colours were strengthened. This was done gradually, to keep a balance between them; finally, darker shadows were put in to the right and below each item, the imaginary light coming from the top left.

Use the above designs for a simpler version of the trompe l'oeil design or to create a border.

LEFT. *Because the chest of drawers and all the projects in this room will have to cope with a lot of wear and tear from their small owner, at least three or four coats of a strong water-based varnish should be applied to each item when it is finished; floor quality would be best, and this should be either satin or gloss so the item can easily be wiped. Alternatively, use an oil-based varnish. Several coats of this may yellow the colours, but you can use three coats of water-based varnish then just one of oil-based.*

To create a chest of drawers like this one, but using your child's favourite toys, arrange these on some book shelves and take a good photograph of the collection from whatever would seem the appropriate eye level. Trace the items, just as was done here, and enlarge them to scale on a photocopier. The photograph will also be a useful guide when you put in the shadows.

LEFT. *This little wardrobe, of brown shiny wood, was sanded with medium sandpaper and given two coats of white acrylic primer/undercoat. The yellow framework was painted in emulsion, overlapping the panels a little, then the panels, in colours matching the chest, but lightened a little with white so the wardrobe wouldn't be overpowering.*

The toy holder, a rigid plastic flowerpot, was rubbed with wet-and-dry paper, and sealed with Unibond and water, followed by acrylic primer/undercoat. Wavy pencil lines were drawn and wobbly stripes painted with emulsions matching the chest; a lining brush was used for the white lines. Finish with at least two coats of varnish.

The outer band and flower on the cushion were hand-painted first in white acrylic primer/undercoat; the border triangles were drawn with pencil and painted with silk paints.

BELOW. This toybox, made from new pine, was sealed in the same way as the chest. It was drawn to scale on paper, in order to plan the size of the windows, doors and roof tiles. The same palette of colours was used as for the chest, so although the design was very different, it blended with the other projects. Having drawn everything on the box, using a pencil and ruler, the roof tiles were painted first. The acrylic paint was put on half of each tile then softened outwards with clean water. Next, the walls were painted with emulsion, and then the details, using acrylic tube colours.

RIGHT. The little table was old pine, so it needed to be de-waxed first. The chair, which was painted with old gloss, was rubbed down with sandpaper. Both were then given two coats of acrylic primer/ undercoat. The design for the table was worked out on paper and drawn on the surface with a pencil. The border was painted first, using the same colours as for the chest, but leaving undercoat in a white line between the squares. The yellow was painted next in emulsion, then all the white lines, including the border ones. A plastic alphabet stencil was used for the letters and a tracing for the flowers. Lastly, the frame and legs were painted, with attractive colour contrasts picked for each section. The chair was painted in the same way, using an enlargement of the tracing on the seat.

GLOSSARY

acrylic primer/undercoat Matt water-based paint bound with acrylic, used for sealing or 'priming' surfaces, or as an undercoat. Can be mixed with any water-based emulsion.

acrylic tube paint Water-based tube paint which, when used in a thick consistency, can imitate oil-paint and, when used in a thin consistency, imitates watercolour. Waterproof when dry.

antiquing General term used to describe methods of achieving an old, antique finish on top of new paint.

badger brush A large specialist brush for softening and blending glaze used for effects such as marbleizing and tortoiseshell.

Blu-tak Putty-like substance, which will stick to any surface; does not harden so is ideal for temporary use.

burnish A rubbing action, either to make a surface smooth, or gilding bright.

casein Glue or paint binder, extracted from the whey of milk.

crackle varnish Cracked, transparent effect created by applying liquid gum arabic over nearly dried 3-hour gold size. The gold size contracts as it continues to dry, causing the cracks in the top coat.

cure Drying until completely hard. This is necessary for oil-based substances and can take up to two weeks, although the surface feels dry after two hours.

distemper Thick, water-based paint, traditionally used for painting ceilings and walls. Bound with casein or egg, making it softer and more absorbent than emulsion.

Dutch metal leaf Imitation gold leaf made from copper and zinc.

emulsion Opaque, water-based wall paint, known as 'latex' in the US.

emulsion glaze Thin, milky, water-based liquid for making transparent, coloured glazes from water-based emulsions, acrylic tube paints or gouache.

fuller's earth A pale dust-coloured powder, available from most chemists, it can be used on oil-based surfaces to break the surface tension and make it accept water-based paints. It can also be mixed with rottenstone and wax for antiquing a carved surface.

gesso (pronounced jesso) Thick, creamy substance made from powdered chalk and rabbit-skin size. Several coats should be applied to a surface and sanded until totally smooth. Used mainly under gilding.

gold size Adhesive used for gilding; it is applied to a surface and the leaf stuck onto it. Available in water-based or oil-based size; the latter can also be used as a varnish, and as the first coat of 'crackle varnish'.

gouache Water-based tube paint, water-soluble when dry, a little thicker and more opaque than watercolour or acrylic paint.

Hammerite Brand name for cellulose-based rustproof paint for metal. Although glossy, it is compatible with water-based glues and varnishes, acrylic paints, and oil-or spirit-based products.

keying Roughening a smooth surface with sandpaper or Wet and Dry paper to help subsequent coats adhere. A coat of PVA glue can be used on glass or china.

liming paste Titanium dioxide white powder pigment, mixed into a soft water-soluble past.

liming wax Titanium dioxide white powder pigment mixed into wax.

liquid gum arabic Liquid gum or glue made from granules of dried sap from trees growing in Arabia. Can be used for sticking and for the top coat of 'crackle varnish'.

low-tack tape Masking tape with a less sticky backing than normal masking tape, ideal for use over a painted surface as it is less likely to damage it.

marbleizing Using a selection of marbling techniques to produce a marble effect in any colour.

marbling Following an exact recipe, both in colours and order of technique, to reproduce the appearance of a true marble, such as Sienna or Verde Antico.

MDF (Medium Density Fibreboard) Ultra-smooth board used in place of wood.

mountboard Thick card used to cut out surrounds or 'mounts' for pictures.

patina Gloss produced by age from polishing or handling a surface.

pigment Pure colour in powder form, soluble in oil-, water- or spirit-based mediums.

Plaka Artists' water-based paint, softer than normal emulsion, and ideal for burnishing.

primary colours Colours - red, blue and yellow - that cannot be mixed from any others.

PVA glue Polyvinyl acetate glue. White when wet, transparent when dry; has a hard but plasticky feel.

rabbit skin size Glue that comes in a dry, granular form; soak overnight in water and warm, use as binder for homemade paint.

rottenstone A dark dust-coloured powder, originally called 'Tripoli', this can be mixed with wax to antique a carved surface, or with linseed oil to create a fine polished agent used in the final stages of varnishing.

runs Unsightly dribbles of paint or varnish, which occur when too much has been applied; difficult to remove when dry so try to avoid them (*see 'sparingly'*).

sanding sealer Methylated spirit- or alcohol-based liquid, fairly matt and almost colourless, normally used for sealing new wood prior to sanding it. Can be used to seal paper prints or, mixed with shellac to deepen the colour, for an antique effect over paint or decoupage.

scumble glaze Oil- or water-based glaze. Slow drying for a textured, transparent, coloured finish on top of paint. Tint oil-based glaze with oil tube paint and water-based glaze with acrylics or emulsion.

secondary colours Colours achieved by mixing equal quantities of two of the primary colours.

shellac Methylated spirit-based lacquer, treacle coloured, good for sealing bare wood and ageing prints or paintwork, giving a honey-coloured tint.

size Normally used for sealing surfaces to make them non-absorbent. Can also refer to glue as in wallpaper size or gold size.

sparingly Dip paintbrush 1/4 to 1/3 of the way up the bristles and, using both sides of the brush in a flip-flop motion, spread the substance as far as possible in all directions as quickly as possible. Smooth over that section with the tips of the bristles in one direction and move on to the middle of the next section and repeat.

'tacky' The surface feels dry when lightly stroked with the fingers, and just sticky when firmly pressed with a knuckle.

tak-rag Thin gauze, impregnated with mixture of oil-based varnish and linseed oil, used to remove fine particles left on painted or varnished surface after sanding, before next coat. Kept in plastic bag or sealed jar when not in use to keep moist.

terracotta A red-brown clay from which garden pots are made; also used to describe a red-brown colour.

tertiary colours Colours achieved by mixing one part of a primary colour with one part of either of its neighbouring secondaries.

transparent lacquer Clear, methylated spirit-based lacquer, also known as French Enamel Varnish. Used as a sealer over gilding; can be mixed with shellac, sanding sealer, white polish and aniline dyes.

tube paint Artists' colours, available in oil, alkyd, acrylic, gouache or watercolour. Oil-based products can be tinted with oil or alkyd tube paints and water-based products with acrylic, gouache or watercolour.

Unibond Brand name of white, water-based glue, bound with polyvinyl acetate. Looks white and creamy when wet, but dries to transparent.

verdigris A grey-green powdery deposit found on copper.

wash Very transparent paint; usually watercolour or acrylic tube paint diluted with lots of water.

wet-and-dry paper Like sandpaper, but more resilient. It is waterproof so can be used with a dampened surface for a better grip.

white polish Methylated spirit- or alcohol-based liquid, similar to French polish.

LIST OF SUPPLIERS

* Mail-order available

UNITED KINGDOM

Ashtree, Unit 37H, Mildmay Grove, London
N1 4RII
Tel. (0171) 359 4696
For liming paste, crackle glaze, specialist brushes.

*Belinda Ballantine, The Abbey Brewery,
Malmesbury, Wiltshire SN16 9AS
Tel. (01666) 822047 Fax (01666) 822293
For small pots of emulsion, crackle varnish, specialist brushes, and unpainted items.

J. W. Bollom and Co., 316 Old Brompton Road,
London SW5 0BP
Tel. (0171) 370 3252
For decorators' merchants supplies.

Coln Gallery, 19 West Market Place,
Cirencester, Gloucestershire GL7 2AE
Tel. (01285) 659085
For artists' and gilding materials, and Plaka.

*Cornelissen and Son Ltd, 105 Great Russell
Street, London WC1B 3RY
Tel. (0171) 636 1045 Fax (0171) 636 3655
For artists' and gilding materials, Plaka, and liquid gum arabic.

*Custom Craft Mouldings, Hollyhill Park,
Cinderford, Gloucestershire GL14 2YB
Tel. (01594) 826623 Fax (01594) 826591
For a wide range of composition mouldings.

*Farrow and Ball, 33 Uddens Trading Estate,
Wimborne, Dorset BH21 7NI
Tel. (01202) 876141
For the National Trust range of period paint colours, including distemper.

*Green and Stone of Chelsea, 259 King's Road,
London SW3 5EL
Tel. (0171) 352 0097 Fax (0171) 351 1098
For artists' and gilding materials, and Plaka.

*Heart of the Country Paints, Home Farm,
Swinfen, Nr. Lichfield, Staffordshire
WS14 9QR
Tel. (01543) 481612
For American buttermilk paints, old colours.

London Graphic Centre, 107–115 Long Acre,
London WC2E 9NT
Tel. (0171) 240 0095 Fax (0171) 831 1544
For waterproof pens, Plaka, ceramic and fabric paints, including silk paints.

Paper and Paints Ltd, 4 Park Walk, London
SW10 0AD
Tel. (0171) 352 8626 Fax (0171) 352 1017
For a range of historic paint colours, and all brushes and materials.

*Pine Brush Products, Coton Clanford,
Stafford ST18 9PB
Tel. (01785) 282 799
For Colourman paints – soft burnishable emulsions in old colours.

*E. Ploton (Sundries) Ltd, 273 Archway Road,
London N6 5AA
Tel. (0181) 348 0315 Fax (0181) 348 3414
For artists' and gilding materials, Plaka, sanding sealer, shellac, and white polish.

Polyvine Ltd, Vine House, Rockhampton,
Berkley, Gloucestershire GL13 9DT
Tel. (01454) 216276
For water-based sealers, varnishes, stains and paints.

Potterton Books, The Old Rectory, Sessay, Nr
Thirsk, North Yorkshire YO7 3LZ
Tel (01845) 401218
For art and reference books, including those out of print.

John Myland Ltd, 80 Norwood High Street,
London SE27 9NW
Tel. (0181) 670 9161 Fax (0181) 761 5700
For waxes, shellac, sanding sealer, white polish, and raw umber emulsion.

Scumble Goosie, 1 Cotswold Place, Chalford
Hill, Stroud, Gloucestershire GL6 8EJ
Tel. (01452) 886414
For unpainted screens, trays, bins and small furniture.

*Stuart R. Stevenson, 68 Clerkenwell Road,
London EC1M 5QA
Tel. (0171) 253 1693 Fax (0171) 490 0451
For artists' and gilding materials.

*Westcountry Finishes Ltd, Unit 4, Station
Business Park, Lower Brimley Ind. Estate,
Teignmouth, Devon TQ14 8QJ
Tel. (01626) 779 994
For water-based sealers, varnishes, stains and paints.

*Wilsons Paints, 40 Fore Street, Exmouth,
Devon EX8 1HU
Tel. (01395) 267 972 Fax (01395) 268 041
For strong emulsion colours especially for furniture, good for mixing your own colours with white or coloured emulsions or as stains.

UNITED STATES

*Pearl Art, Craft and Graphic Discount
Centers; branches at all the following
addresses:
308 Canal Street, NY, NY 10013
Tel. (212) 431 7932 and 1 800 221 6845 Fax
(212) 274 8290. Orders: Pearl by Mail 1-800-
451-Pearl (7327)
2411 Hempstead Tpke, East Meadow, NY
11544
Tel. (516) 731 3700 Fax (516) 731 3721.
Orders: 516 579 6450
776 Route 17N, Paramus, NJ 07652
Tel. (201) 447 0300 Fax (201) 447 4102
6000 Route 1, Woodbridge, New Jersey, 07095
Tel. (908) 634 9400 Fax (908) 634 6851
2100 Route 38, Cherry Hill, New Jersey 08002
Tel. (609) 667 6500 Fax (609) 667 6249
579 Massachusetts Avenue, Cambridge,
Massachusetts 02139
Tel. (617) 547 6600 Fax (617) 547 1906
12266 Rockville Pike, Suite P, Rockville,
Maryland 20852
Tel. (301) 816 2900 Fax (301) 816 4955
5695 Telegraph Road, Alexandria, Virginia
22303
Tel. (703) 960 3900 Fax (703) 960 9130
3756 Roswell Road, Atlanta, Georgia 30342
Tel. (404) 233 9400 Fax (404) 841 0382
1033 East Oakland Park Boulevard, Ft.
Lauderdale, Florida 33334
Tel. (305) 564 5700 Fax (305) 564 5715
4539 West Kennedy Boulevard, Tampa,
Florida 33609
Tel. (813) 286 8000 Fax (813) 286 0621
1140 East Altamonte Drive, Altamonte
Springs, Florida 32701
Tel. (407) 831 9000 Fax (407) 831 1042
6448 South Dixie Highway, South Miami,
Florida 33143
Tel. (305) 663 8899 Fax (305) 663 8382
6100 Westheimer Road, Suite 142A, Houston,
Texas 77057
Tel. (713) 977 5600 Fax (713) 977 4968
For a wide range of art supplies.

AUSTRALIA

The Folk Art Studio, 200 Pittwater Road,
Manly, NSW 2095
Tel. (02) 977 7091
For a wide range of craft materials including wooden items.

*Janet's Art Supplies, 145 Victoria Avenue,
Chatswood 2067, Sydney
Tel. (02) 417 8572 Fax (02) 417 7617
For a wide range of general art supplies.

*Oxford Art Supplies Pty Ltd, 221–223 Oxford
Street, Darlinghurst 2010, Sydney
Tel. (02) 360 4066 Fax (02) 360 3461
For general art supplies.

INDEX

FURTHER READING

Cavelle, Simon. *The Encyclopedia of Decorative Paint effects*, London, Headline, 1994

de Dampierre, Florence. *The Best of Painted Furniture*, London, Wiedenfeld & Nicholson, 1987

Decorative Painting of the World, London, Ebury Press, 1993

Ellingsgard, Nils. *Norwegian Rose Painting*, Oslo, Det Norske Samlaget, 1988

Guegan, Yannick. *Frises et Ornements*, Paris, Dessain et Tolva, 1993

Innes, Jocasta. *Scandinavian Painted Decor*, London, Cassell, 1994

Mayer, Ralph. *The Artists' Handbook of Materials and Techniques*, London, Faber &

Faber, 1951

McCloud, Kevin. *Kevin McCloud's Decorating Book*, London, Dorling Kindersley, 1990

Miller, Margaret M. & Aarseth Sigmund. *Norwegian Rosemaling*, New York, Charles Scribner's Sons, 1974

Ness, Annie. *Restaurering avbygdemøbler*, Oslo, Landbruksforlaget, 1988

O'Neil, Isobel. *The Art of the Painted Finish for Furniture and Decoration*, New York, William Morrow Company Inc., 1971

Pietersen, Wil & Venekamp, Leidy. *The Hindeloopen Painter's Guide*, Amsterdam, Detille Leeuwarden, 1983

Rees, Yvonne. *The Decorative Artist*, London, Headline, 1988

Rhodes, Brian & Windsor, John. *Parry's Graining and Marbling*, London, Collins, 1949

Ritz, Gislind M. *The Art of Painted Furniture*, New York, van Nostrand Reinhold, 1970

Ritz, Joseph M. & Gislind. *Alte bemalke Bauernmöbel*, Munich, Verlag Georg D. W. Callweg, 1975

Rust, Graham. *The Painted House*, London, Cassell, 1991

Sloane, Annie & Gwynn, Kate. *The Complete Book of Decorative Paint Techniques*, London, Century Hutchinson, 1988

Waring, Janet. *Early American Stencils on Walls and Furniture*, New York, Dover Publications, 1968

AUTHOR'S ACKNOWLEDGEMENTS

For the second time, my enormous thanks to all at Eddison Sadd Editions for having the confidence in me to ask me to write another book: to Ian, Zoë, Elaine, Karen and Pritty; and to my old friend, Diana Lodge, for so kindly agreeing to edit it for me. A special thank you to Sue Atkinson for her beautiful photographs, and to her assistant, Mario, whose ingenuity knows no bounds, both tolerating with laughter and patience almost impossible angles and fusing lights. For the locations, my huge thanks to Angela and Bill Sykes and Isobel and Tim Coulson, who allowed us to invade their homes and transform several of their rooms, giving us always the warmest of welcomes for days on end, and to Paul von Fullman, for allowing us to use two rooms in his beautiful restaurant, Fullman's at Crudwell, near Malmesbury.

To MFI Furniture for wonderful kitchen units; to Texas Home Care for the kitchen chairs and the breakfast room table; to Scumble Goosie for the study wastepaper bin, and to Rene Nicholls Antiques for inspiring the colour scheme of the child's room.

My greatest thanks of all go to my assistants, Sally Richmond and Ann Witchell, who with unfailing willingness and energy helped me to paint all the projects in time to meet what sometimes seemed like impossible deadlines! Without their enormous support and help, this book could not have been painted. Very great thanks also, to the extra helping hands of Helen Richmond, Ava Chance and Eric Witchell.

EDDISON-SADD EDITIONS

Project Editor	Zoë Hughes
Copy-editor	Diana Lodge
Indexer	Dorothy Frame
Art Director	Elaine Partington
Designers	Karen Watts and Pritty Ramjee
Line Illustrations	Anthony Duke
Production	Hazel Kirkman and Charles James

Photographs on pages 8 and 9 are reproduced courtesy of Bonhams London/ Bridgeman Art Library.